A Celebration of Clematis

A Celebration of Clematis

By Kaye Heafey and Ron Morgan

Photography by Keith Lewis

Half Full Press · Oakland, CA

For information, contact

Half Full Press

1814 Franklin Street, Suite 815

Oakland, CA 94612

(510) 839-5471

Editing/Design by Angie Hinh

10 09 08 07 06   1 2 3 4 5

ISBN 0-9719552-6-3

Printed and bound in China

A special thank you to Angie Hinh for her talent and quiet dedication. We couldn't have completed this book in record time without her.

For my husband Richard,
"the wind beneath my wings."

Contents

Foreword

My association with Chalk Hill Clematis dates back a few years. When I first visited in May 2003 at the invitation of its manager, Murray Rosen, what impressed me and aroused my curiosity most was the unusually long and straight flower stems of Clematis *x durandii* – a fine herbaceous plant universally loved and widely grown by gardeners, and clematophiles in particular. Having been informed that Chalk Hill Clematis specializes in growing and shipping clematis as cut flowers, it did not take long for me to realize that it must be a very special nursery with some magical formula to produce such long-stemmed, perfect flowers. Inspection of the extensive nursery with its rows and rows of different varieties of carefully grown clematis in full flower confirmed my thoughts. I was in my element, overjoyed by the fact that this very special and versatile genus of plants was being grown to such perfection in a county more noted for its extensive vineyards producing excellent wines.

Then I met Kaye Heafey, the owner of Chalk Hill Clematis. She enthusiastically shared with me her vision and future plans for the flower farm and nursery. One of her goals was to establish a proper clematis display garden for gardeners to glean ideas for selecting and growing clematis in their own gardens. As someone who has enjoyed gardening with clematis for over thirty-five years, I was delighted to be invited to participate in making this goal a reality.

In a short time, a suitable site for the display garden was carefully selected away from mature and spreading oak trees. I was given the task of designing it, a daunting prospect, but the importance of a clematis display garden, open to the public – my life long dream – enabled me to embark on this project with great gusto. My design and planting schemes for the new garden were carefully studied, interpreted, modified where necessary, and executed most efficiently by Murray. Kaye's enthusiastic support, encouragement, and financial input turned plans into reality. The Mary Toomey Clematis Garden at Chalk Hill Clematis was officially opened to the public in May 2006.

A Celebration of Clematis, the story of Chalk Hill Clematis, celebrates the completion of this ambitious project and gives an overview of the story of farm and clematis nursery. I hope that all those who acquire a copy of this delightful book will be persuaded to visit Chalk Hill Clematis. See the gardens within a large garden, admire the amazing range of clematis growing, and of course meet its friendly manager, Murray Rosen, and his staff. Your journey will be well worthwhile – you may even be tempted to take home a clematis plant or two to enjoy in your own gardens and bring into your homes.

Gertrude Jekyll, most celebrated English gardener, wrote in *Home and Garden* in 1900, "It always seems to me that one of the things most worth doing about a garden is to try to make every part of it beautiful." I second this unreservedly and add that clematis as a garden plant will not only make every part of your garden beautiful, Clematis as a cut flower will also make every part of your home beautiful. Such is the versatility of the genus Clematis.

Mary Toomey

Introduction

My love of flowers traces back to my childhood. Growing up in Wyoming, I was uniquely attracted to nature, flowers, and floral arranging. My mother is a beautiful gardener, loves her garden, and has a wonderful herbaceous border. Even in my teens, I used to cut flowers from her garden and make small arrangements in the house – I never lost this interest. All the women in my family love things of beauty; they have what is termed a "good eye."

So, this is the way I grew up; I then left home, majored in art history, and continued the development of my own good eye. With my marriage to Richard came our three wonderful children, Brendan, Caroline, and Austin. Now, I'm enjoying my grandson Henry.

This book details the next chapter in my life, the story behind Chalk Hill Clematis. Creating it has been an ongoing adventure. Richard always said I have energy, imagination, focus – fixation even – and am a driving force. But none of this would have been possible without love and friendship too. Like the colorful vines that we grow, threads of friendships twine through the following pages, helping bind our story. A shared interest in flower arranging inspired my friendship with floristry expert Carrie Glenn. Her wish list for flowering vines to use in her designs kick-started our whole project.

Ron Morgan and I have been friends for many years. We share passions for flowers, antiques, and art. It was Ron who saw the potential in our flowers to make a real impact on the East Coast. He personally transported a hundred bunches of our clematis and used them to such great effect in his floral displays commissioned for a big New York wedding. They were a sensation, the bride was entranced, and the word went out amongst the floral designers. So our market became firmly established.

Murray Rosen, our farm manager, has been a tower of strength from the earliest days of Chalk Hill Clematis. He developed our idea and was so important in turning it into reality. Throughout our long relationship, we have equally shared our successes and failures.

What started out as a conversation between friends about the dearth of field-grown floral material grew first into a specialty cut flower farm business. From there, our clematis nursery seemed to grow naturally. Over the years, we've all gained in experience. This year we've added the Mary Toomey Clematis Garden – a garden that displays the versatility of clematis in a natural setting, grown amongst trees, flowering shrubs, roses, and sculpture.

And now to the writing of this book about Chalk Hill Clematis. Once again, I have to thank Ron for another idea in the history of our project. "Why not write a book – and I'll create some beautiful floral displays with your wonderful clematis. Let's just do this together!"

So here it is – the story of Chalk Hill Clematis. I hope you enjoy reading all about us.

Kaye Heafey

Even as a very little child I loved flowers. I grew up in Stockton, California, but I spent every summer back in Iowa with my grandparents. I really loved being outside, working in my grandmother's garden with her. It was like a love affair with nature, plants, and flowers. Especially flowers – I loved to pick them and make arrangements inside. At ten years old, I won my first flower show competition in San Joaquin County, California. I always knew I was going to end up working with flowers. It was as simple as that for me.

In college, I trained to be an art school teacher, and this gave me a good feeling for space, light, color, and scale – all these fundamental principles that apply to painting and sculpture also apply to floral design. As an artist, I always wanted to do my version of art with flowers. They are my medium.

After college, I spent three years in London creating window displays for Harrods. There, I discovered Pulbrook & Gould florists on Sloane Street. In its heyday, it was the most fabulous flower shop in the world. Lady Pulbrook and Miss Gould put displays together in a riotous way – I just loved what they were doing and went there to work part time. Boundaries were blurred between rare blooms and nature. Mixed herbs that you thought were for cooking were arranged into exquisite bunches that completely outclassed regular bouquet flowers like lilies and carnations. A trailing stem of blackberries made the perfect companion to the deepest, darkest roses you can find – it was fabulous.

After that, I moved back close to home, settling in the East Bay, where I've been ever since. While working as an art teacher, in my spare time I also worked for a florist producing other people's designs. With my flair for color and love of all shapes and sizes of flowers, I thought, "I can do this – I can design with flowers better than this." I started working for friends, then their friends, so clients built up. It snowballed from there. Now, I have a warehouse for creating displays and two antique shops – they work together, almost like a package deal.

Today, I spend six months of the year on the road, lecturing to garden clubs all over the country.

I've always loved clematis. But I'm a flower arranger, not a gardener, on the run twelve to fifteen hours a day, so I only grow about fifteen or so clematis in my own garden. That's all I can handle: enough to use in my own home. For large commissions, I need more than handfuls.

Life's about working with friends. Kaye and I have been friends for a very long time. Her production levels at Chalk Hill had reached a point where she could supply me with the quantity of flowers to make a real impact at a huge society wedding I was about to do in New York. How serendipitous! I asked her to cut me some bunches and took them with me. I used hundreds of large, all white Clematis 'Henryi' everywhere in naturalistic displays with grape vines: the bride's bouquet, table displays, everywhere. So many clematis blooms, people couldn't believe their eyes. Next day, all the wholesale florists in New York called me to ask where I got such fabulous flowers. The rest is history.

This is my third book, and the first co-authored. I've been very lucky – life has been exceptionally good to me. My life working with flowers has been a case of right place, right time, right occasion. It felt completely natural to say to Kaye, "Let's do a book together."

Ron Morgan

The Property | 1

The beauty of Chalk Hill Clematis starts with its location. It's off the beaten track, tucked among the oak-studded hills of Sonoma County – a beautiful part of California's wine country, as well as the perfect place for family vacations. We liked the agrarian feel of the property, which is why we bought it in 1981. It was a relaxing place to escape from the frenetic pace of life in the San Francisco Bay Area. From the start, we wanted our property to be agricultural in some way. But we also wanted to keep most of the acreage natural, blending right into the surrounding rolling landscape.

Just over ten years later, around 1992, our thoughts became more focused on how our acreage could be made more productive. Vineyards surround Chalk Hill, adding green stripes to the hillsides in summer when the grassland all around has been turned golden by the sun. Early on, viniculture was rejected – we agreed that we wanted to produce something more unusual than wine. Our wild kingdom, as we call it, provides a wonderful native habitat fairly teeming with deer, wild boar, coyotes, turkeys, rattlesnakes, rabbits, and the occasional visiting cow.

All kinds of products and produce were considered and discarded, including farming wild boar, chickens, and eggs. Like many other good ideas, Chalk Hill Clematis grew out of a chance exchange between friends. Renowned floristry expert Carrie Glenn had become well known in the area partly through her work at the restaurant Chez Panisse in Berkeley. As regular diners there, the connection between the two of us was made.

Carrie generously shared some of her designer's sources and trade secrets. Her spectacular, naturalistic displays included a range of flowers and foraged materials – twigs, lichen covered branches, berries, cones, leaves, seedheads, and wild flowers – plants that might be considered weeds by some. All this Carrie found in her early morning searches at the San Francisco flower mart. Getting there incredibly early was essential in order to find the best of the most unusual, sometimes wildly exuberant, and therefore highly prized, foraged materials.

Carrie's eclectic approach to floral design is similar to that of Constance Spry (1886-1960), an English florist, designer, teacher, and social reformer. Spry became well known as a society florist and best-selling author who understood the power of flowers not only to beautify homes, but to lift the spirits of creators and family members alike. In the mid-20th century, she taught millions of Britons how easy it was to bring beauty into their homes with wild flowers and accessible materials literally plucked from hedgerows and found on wasteland. Spry liberated people's imaginations from what constituted "suitable" floral material, while broadening their horizons as to where to find this cornucopia. She taught that there were rich pickings to be discovered everywhere; foraging knew no boundaries, from the hedgerows, open fields, and roadsides of the country to the urban wastelands and vegetable patches on the outskirts of towns and cities. Spry also taught her followers not to let convention restrict their choice of vases in which to create exuberant floral displays. It was a case of no crystal, no problem – elegance and beauty could be displayed in a variety of vessels. Spry's signature style included the use of containers ranging from kitchen baking trays, sauce boats, and tureen lids to the more esoteric birdcages, huge shells, and hollowed tree trunk sections.

Like Spry, Carrie loves to work in a naturalistic way. It was easy to find blossoming shrubs and roses, climbers, and other interesting foraged materials to partner with cut flowers. But there was a complete dearth of flowering vines to bring an exuberant flow to her floral designs. This gap in the market became the focus of our discussion. Out of this, the original concept of Chalk Hill Clematis evolved. From the outset, we wanted field-grown materials – clematis, other vines, and shrubs. The aim was to present unpretentious flowers, ideal for curvaceous, naturalistic displays, all unlike the rigid formality of hothouse flowers. Field-grown flowers retain a closeness to nature and are not uniform specimens. Talking about it like that, with infectious enthusiasm for an idea, all seemed achievable. And the timing seemed right. From many perspectives, clematis made a natural choice in which to specialize.

Our product would be high-quality, unusual cut flowers and we would sell direct. The business plan – ours because no other existed – was non-traditional and flexible of necessity. It took time and a lot of research and development before we were close to a tangible product. Patience and drive were also required to get the idea behind Chalk Hill Clematis off the ground, literally.

Carrie was hired as our consultant, but was clear about the fact that her involvement would be limited to the initial stages. Early on in this process of creating Chalk Hill Clematis, Carrie passed the baton back, but not before she had introduced Murray Rosen to us. His charter: to nurture and manage our project.

A friend of Carrie's, Murray is an artist by training, and thus also possesses a "good eye." After training as a sculptor at the School of Sculpture and Design in New York, he changed track, having fallen under the spell of roses. Since mastering horticulture through apprenticeships at nurseries, he was specializing in roses at a Bay Area nursery. In many ways, the cultivation and care of roses and clematis are similar. Murray has proven to be an excellent manager and his depth of knowledge has been central to the development and success of the business. Not only has he managed the project, he has also constantly refined the product, based on observation and knowledge.

By spring 1994, Murray and I were faced with the monumental task of actually creating Chalk Hill Clematis. Starting with basics, a road had to be put in to access the site. Next, fencing to keep wildlife away from the plants, and then a proper growing environment had to be created out of an uncultivated area. Netting was installed to provide filtered shade from the sun in half of the growing field. At this point, no plants had been purchased for the farm. So we worked on making plant selections, planting the many plants required, and getting them growing. We also faced a mountain of refinement.

Progress was slow. With no pattern to follow, it was almost a case of reinventing the uninvented. Dutch growers had done some work with Clematis x *durandii* for cutting, but nothing like what we were about to do in a field situation.

It became increasingly evident that clematis was a gem that many people wanted. It was the right product, with its varied flower forms ranging from large, bold saucer-style flowers to miniature, delicate pitcher shapes. Combined with this, its color spectrum fans out from elegant, pristine whites to saturated jewel box, highly valued shades.

But if clematis was an obvious choice, which varieties to grow was not. And where to get the plants, how to grow them to produce straight stems, when was the perfect harvest time – the list of challenges was long. Add to this other problems of conditioning, packaging, and distribution, and what started out as a "simple" project became increasingly complex. But despite all this, the feeling that "we can do this" remained strong.

Eventually, fifteen acres of the property became dedicated to this vision. Other essentials followed: a barn, coolers, hundreds of different clematis varieties, magnificent climbing and rambling roses – in all, thousands of plants were selected, acquired, and descended on Chalk Hill.

Being in the position to introduce an exciting new product to the market was a source of great pride and pleasure. Getting that product to the market, however, was yet another hurdle. Initially, it was a case of marketing by phone and personal contact. Hands-on marketing literally meant just that. A drive up to Chalk Hill from the Bay Area, followed by cutting and bunching flowers, then loading up the station wagon before driving the first bunches of our cut clematis to one of our first customers, Bloomers Florist, a premier floral business in San Francisco. Word about the new cut flowers spread to other specialty designers throughout northern California and our local fame grew.

As an unexpected bonus, national fame came surprisingly early through the efforts of Ron Morgan. A friend for many years, we share a passion for flowers, antiques, and art. He's always so enthusiastic. Seeing something different and new – clematis as a cut flower – Ron insisted on personally transporting a hundred bunches from Chalk Hill Clematis to New York to use them in his floral displays for a large wedding commission. Clematis were used everywhere, from the bride's elegant bouquet to magnificent table displays. They proved to be a Broadway-style smash hit and caused a sensation. Not only was the bride ecstatic, other New York designers demanded to know his source. Calls flooded in from wholesale florists and FedEx boxes of clematis flew out of the barn door.

So Chalk Hill Clematis was born and developed into a first-class, specialty cut flower farm. We planted a large array of flowering trees, shrubs, rambling and English roses to complement the clematis. From just five or six clematis varieties grown for cutting in the first couple of years, we steadily added more, reaching over forty today.

Clematis is an occasion flower – a perfect choice for weddings. In the beginning, thinking that weddings were going to be our main market, we only produced white flowers. Back then, floral designers were asked exclusively for white blooms for weddings. As time went on, however, we gradually realized that there was a great demand for the amazing deep saturated color palette of lilac, blues, cerise, and purples that clematis offer.

Once our cut flower business was under control, we looked for ways to extend our season, adding another source of income to increase our commercial viability. A clematis nursery seemed a logical addition to the flower farm. So, our nursery specializing in clematis came to be. Chalk Hill Clematis now ships hundreds of different clematis plants across the country. We went online in 1999 (www.chalkhillclematis.com) and now sell almost solely through the Web. The South and East, with their large gardens, have proved our biggest markets to date.

It's been a learning process for everyone, but a very satisfying, worthwhile one. Today, Chalk Hill Clematis is run by an exceptional team of individuals, all adding their expertise to a successful endeavor. I remain as passionately involved in our business as I was right at the start, when Carrie Glenn provided the catalyst, a germ of an idea. Murray helped make it all happen. On the cut flower side, Miguel and Maria are brilliant with flowers; Miguel is excellent at staggering the crop of blooms by cutting back at exactly the right intervals of time. Fernando and Arturo take care of the nursery and property, plus we have a contractor in the spring to do some additional seasonal work. Jennifer keeps our office running smoothly. Now this year, Mary Toomey's new garden has rounded out our business.

At Chalk Hill, we grow clematis as field-grown, specialty cut flowers. How it was done is our story. Although clematis has been long-valued and written about as a garden flower, there was no reference explaining how to encourage them to stand up straight enough to make a suitable cut flower. Grown as a cut flower, clematis never entirely lose their natural suppleness. That's a large part of the appeal of clematis; this airy architectural elegance, combined with the profusion of jewel box colors that makes them irresistible to floral designers.

We faced many challenges at Chalk Hill. It took time to develop our concept and overcome these challenges. Along the way, we learned from our failures as well as our successes. Being field-grown, our flowers have health and hardiness built in. Growth is subject to the natural seasonal fluctuations of temperature and rainfall that occur in our part of northern California. We are in a Mediterranean climate zone, with dry, hot summers followed by wet, relatively warm winters. Clematis, however delicate they may appear, are hardy and not as sensitive to weather fluctuations as other cut flowers, such as roses. And, as cut flowers, they have longer lives than roses; they last up to two weeks, making them clear winners in this important aspect.

We have refined how we grow our plants over the years, adapting our methods as we learned more about what works best. To create large vigorous plants with many stems, each one must be cut back several times a year to encourage new growth and flowers. With large flowered clematis, this happens two or three times a year, producing a new flush of blooms. For herbaceous cultivars, cutting back takes place five or six times in a season. The problem is getting the clematis to come back

with vigor, but our staff has become expert at this. We tell designers and customers that the largest flowers are produced in spring. As the season progresses, the number of stems in each bunch is increased to allow for the slightly smaller flowers.

In the beginning, we tried to cut the clematis when in bloom, rather than in bud. Although they are tough, we soon learned that cutting in bud is best. All stems are conditioned straight after cutting. Buckets go everywhere with Miguel and Maria as they work. Once cut, stems are immediately plunged into water. They make multiple trips up to the barn with full buckets; flowers are transferred to another solution and kept in the cooler until ready for dispatch. Happily, we used a version of this technique to hold clematis for about four weeks for our daughter's wedding two years ago. Water was changed regularly while they were in storage and they looked absolutely spectacular on the wedding day.

The herbaceous group of clematis tends to be undervalued in many ways. But home gardeners and flower arrangers keen to grow their own clematis for cutting should start off looking at this group. They are so easy to grow, produce a strong stem, and are much easier to support than the large flower climbing varieties. Grow them very simply, using a tomato form, or gathered with twine around the stems. It's become something of a mission at Chalk Hill Clematis to encourage gardeners to be more adventurous in the ways they plant and grow all forms of clematis.

In 1998, the clematis nursery was started as a companion

business to our specialty cut flowers. This original business was established by then and already attracting national attention from designers, wholesalers in the flower market, and the media. Starting the clematis nursery was a natural development and made sound business sense. We had the expertise and credibility, as growers and gardeners were already calling us for advice on how to grow clematis. We started in a very modest fashion, offering only a handful of varieties primarily as a wholesaler to regional nurseries.

A year later, the development of the Chalk Hill Clematis website (www.chalkhillclematis.com) launched us into cyberspace, transforming the nursery into a national internet retail provider. Since then, the nursery has established itself as one of the premier clematis nurseries in the USA, currently offering over 300 varieties and shipping to gardeners in forty-nine of the fifty states – Hawaii being the only exception. Our goal from the beginning was to offer a selection of clematis not available at most nurseries, to produce plants with well-developed root systems that were large enough to plant directly in the garden, and to offer expert advice to customers regarding the care and selection of clematis for their gardens.

We sought out the rare, unusual, and beautiful varieties and imported them from various small growers around the world – there is a lot of interesting hybridization work going on. To produce the size of plant we wanted, we looked beyond the standard industry pot sizes used for clematis growing and experimented with a long, narrow tree pot. This was perfect, giving us just the right type of plant we wanted, and has become a signature of the nursery. To paraphrase the late Jim Fisk, who had one of finest clematis nurseries in England and has been a role model for us, clematis are all about the roots, and if you give the customer a plant with a well-developed root system, they will have success. To ensure our plants arrive at their destinations in good condition despite rough handling beyond our control, we brought in an expert box maker to develop a custom box to suit the size of our container and guarantee the stability of the plants during shipping.

Producing a well-grown plant at a reasonable cost is paramount at Chalk Hill. Offering great plant choices is another important goal.

Although our team is small, we have always placed great attention and importance on customer service. Farm manager and clematis expert Murray Rosen still answers the many questions that come into the nursery, ensuring that our customers get the very best advice possible about caring for their plants and helping in their plant selections. The nursery continues to add to its holdings each year with new plants coming from Japan, Poland, Estonia, Ukraine, and the United Kingdom. In addition, we are resurrecting older cultivars and varieties that are still garden-worthy and should not be forgotten.

Today, Chalk Hill Clematis is a flower farm and clematis nursery of distinction.

In addition, both olive oil and balsamic vinegar are produced on the estate. The oil is a blend of Spanish "Manzanillo" and Italian varietals of olive trees that were originally planted to landscape the area around the barn. Serendipitously, we discovered they produced a very bountiful crop. Our first crop was pressed, bottled, and taken to a tasting. To our great surprise, it won an award. Being a small-scale operation, olive oil production remains incidental to the main part of our business. Chalk Hill olive oil is only sold through our website and directly from the farm.

Balsamic vinegar naturally complements olive oil. Ours is made in an authentic acetaia built at Chalk Hill. Renowned chef Paul Bertolli manages the process of making the vinegar and cares for it in a battery of wooden barrels coopered in a variety of woods imported from Italy. These casks add a complexity to the vinegar. Like our olive oil, Chalk Hill balsamic vinegar is available only through our website and directly from the farm.

The Flowers | 3

The theatricality of all plants speaks to me and I love using them to create magnificent displays that make a lasting impact. I tell my lecture audiences not to be intimidated — always let your materials speak to you. And listen to them! That's the best advice I can give anyone. Flower arranging is like creating landscapes on furniture. You're in charge of the whole kit and caboodle — the features and focal points are your choice of containers and flowers, and you scale your designs to match your home setting and accessories.

I've always loved clematis; they have such a great range of flower shapes and colors. The shapes and coloring are so subtle and sophisticated, with such great form, too. I love all the creamy white cultivars, the ones with delicate veining in particular, and the delicate peachy-pink flowering types. I am more in tune with a single petal flower; to me it's more interesting than a double — you can see the substance of it. Clematis is one of the prettiest single flowers of them all. Add to this its other qualities that, to me, make it more versatile than a rose.

Discovering that Chalk Hill Clematis was producing clematis as cut flowers was like manna from heaven. It was serendipitous that my old friend Kaye was its author.

After clematis flowers pass, many have wonderful seedheads, all furry texture and fuzziness, in subtle shades of beige, taupe, and bronze. Just great! As they're producing something interesting for around nine months of the year, there is a longer time frame in which to use them. In California, we get flowers from different types for about the same time. It's almost the same in colder zones, as there are clematis cultivars that bloom naturally in winter months. I prefer things in season, not forced, hothouse flowers. I don't want to see irises twelve months of the year. But I'm very happy to be able to work with clematis for nine months of the year.

Using various forms of clematis, all from Chalk Hill, along with an assorted collection of containers and settings, I demonstrate in this chapter the infinite variations and possibilities that clematis provide.

Give your imagination free reign and let the clematis do its job. Listen to your flowers, don't worry about the details, have fun and go for it. Let's play together and celebrate clematis.

Ron Morgan

Ron's Tips For Clematis as a Cut Flower

Chalk Hill Clematis takes as good care with their cut flowers as you are ever going to find. They are the best you can get your hands on. Here are some of my tips to help you get the best out of clematis in your arrangements.

The Prep

- Use a sharp knife – no clippers – to re-cut the stems. Take off half an inch in a clean diagonal cut to ensure that the maximum amount of water is available to the flowers.

- Keep stems in lukewarm water – this helps them take the maximum amount of fluid into their system so it goes right up to the head. It gets the circulation of fluid going through the stems.

- Leave stems in warm water for a couple of hours – about two or three – until you are ready to use them and keep the container out of direct sunlight. The water will become room temperature.

The Info

- Clematis are great mixers; they work well with many other flowers. They are adaptable and can be used in either informal or more formal displays. If I am using them with other materials, I prefer to mix clematis with flowers that bloom at the same time of year outside. What looks natural outside works best in arrangements inside. Roses make great display companions with clematis. In my garden, I grow clematis on an arbor with roses.

- When using clematis in mixed arrangements, I prefer to combine them with other flowers in softer shades of color, not from the brighter side of the palette. For me, oranges and strong reds don't work with clematis – such bright colors dominate and take over a display. Again, roses in the softer shades make a classic partner for clematis flowers.

- For fall and holiday displays, embrace the versatility of clematis. Use the wonderful seedheads produced by many clematis species and cultivars.

The Display

- Try to create your clematis display in place; it helps with getting the scale just right. Avoid bright and direct sun – it takes too much energy out of plants and they'll never last as long.

- Use as simple a container as possible. Glass and simple ceramics are the best. I try to avoid metal of any type – most give off oxides, which will sometimes kill flowers. Flowers give off their own oxides and these mix with any from a metal container, so they won't last as well. Use a plain glass or ceramic vessel as a liner for a good metal container that makes a perfect foundation for a display.

- Containers do not have to be expensive. Dime stores have great finds. A clean, simple shape is better than a lot of ornamentation. I love groupings of containers, for example using four or five containers down a table, or in groups on top of a buffet.

- Fill containers with clean water, leaving space for the stems to displace without causing an overflow.

- Scale height and shape of a display to its position. For a buffet table, some height works, but for a sit down dinner, either keep it down low, or above head height of seated guests. Or keep arrangements light and airy so that you can see through them – conversation is important. Clematis are brilliant in this respect – so airy and their twining vine quality allows you to see through them. Their flowers fill out space without appearing heavy.

- Clematis don't work well with holding methods such as floral foam. They have to go straight into water. Unlike roses, carnations, or gardenia, they don't work well as a bare stem bloom on a table. Having water around their stems is essential.

- Decorative glass beads and pebbles work well with clematis, but don't let them crush the stems. The biggest mistake to make is to force clematis into doing something they don't do naturally. It's best to let their stems do what they want to do – hang, fall, drape. They fall beautifully and their informality is what makes them so gorgeous in the first place – it can't be improved. Go with the flow and the natural look.

- Remove leaves that fall below the water line. Foliage rots in water and shortens the lives of all flowers.

The Aftercare

- Clematis flowers will last two weeks. Refresh water. I recommend changing it every other day. A turkey baster helps make this practical: use it to draw water out and top up with fresh water.

- Good clean water is the very best thing for all cut flowers, including clematis. Where a regular complete change of water is not practical, add a tablespoon of bleach to each gallon of water. It helps keep water bacteria-free. Flower stems produce bacteria as they take in oxygen from water – it makes a scum on the surface that not only smells, but causes the flowers to degenerate faster.

- Resist the urge to sweep away fallen clematis petals – use them as part of your arrangement; leave them lying on the table. This is what nature does. Passing glory has it's own beauty and there is still a wonderful center to each flower. Don't dismantle the whole arrangement. Just enjoy the clematis flowers while they are here. You will never see the exact same arrangement again. That's what is so wonderful about nature. Enjoy the moment now.

The Mary Toomey Garden | 4

Dr. Mary Toomey, author of many books, including *The Illustrated Encyclopedia of Clematis*, lecturer, broadcaster, and world-renowned clematis authority, was invited by farm manager Murray Rosen to visit Chalk Hill in May 2003. She had expressed great interest in the nursery, and was able to fit a visit into her schedule while traveling to the Pacific Northwest from her home in Dublin, Ireland.

Mary visited for an entire day, and was interested and surprised to see the work we were doing with clematis as a specialty cut flower. The large selection of plants offered by our nursery also impressed her. At the end of her visit, a new friendship had been forged, together with an agreement to develop a clematis display garden for which she would provide the design.

Mary was truly the inspiration behind the new display garden that bears her name. Like her, we at Chalk Hill believe a demonstration garden is essential to show the public the versatility of the genus Clematis. Clematis enhance and extend the blooming season in any garden and make the perfect companion plant for roses, trees, and shrubs. The large array of herbaceous types in particular offers a rich seam of plants, easy to grow for all gardeners, even the less experienced. Our display garden demonstrates this and encourages gardeners to be more experimental in the use of clematis in their gardens.

The opening of the garden was set for the spring of 2006. Although three years sounds like a long time, in garden-making terms it is just "minutes." A lot had to happen in a very short period of time, and nobody knew back then that Spring 2006 would be one of the wettest and coolest on record. But then, as gardeners, we should all be used to the vagaries of the weather.

The Mary Toomey Clematis Garden, as we named it, is a garden within a garden. It sits alongside the nursery, all set against the backdrop of the beautiful hills of northern California. Mary took charge of the design of the garden. She envisioned a large pergola planted with climbing roses and clematis in the new garden, with a strong central feature, a gazebo serving as the main axis point around which five separate gardens would be created, each with a different theme. We all wanted the garden to both educate and to inspire, allowing visitors to see clematis combined with other perennials, shrubs, and trees in a real garden setting, in addition to being grown as specimens on various structures and tuteurs, as they are more commonly seen.

With Mary back home in Dublin, there was constant communication between Murray and me about design elements and plant combinations. As garden plans developed over the next two years, we had to modify Mary's plant selections to accommodate the hot, dry, Mediterranean climate at Chalk Hill. We wrestled with the "problem"

the various geometric elements from garden to garden would act as a unifying feature that ties the five gardens together despite each having a different theme. So the Mary Toomey Clematis Garden at Chalk Hill evolved from plans and plant lists to a living demonstration of clematis enhancements to garden design. As the garden developed, Murray literally gave life to Mary's design.

All five gardens interest and inspire gardeners. The eighty-foot long herbaceous bed is perhaps the most influential area. It is dedicated to the late British gardener and garden writer Christopher Lloyd, who perfected the design and planting of similarly huge borders at his garden, Great Dixter, in East Sussex, England. In our large herbaceous bed, we feature the non-clinging, shrub-like herbaceous varieties of clematis mixed into classic perennial planting, set between a border of Nepeta 'Walker's Low' in the front and Philadelphus 'Avalanche' in the rear.

Mary and all of us at Chalk Hill Clematis want a visit to this garden to be an inspiration for gardeners, to encourage them to expand their knowledge and make more use of all varieties of clematis. The herbaceous group of clematis is incredibly useful and dynamic, so full of potential. It is still relatively unknown to most American gardeners and we hope this garden will help promote an appreciation of the many attributes of the herbaceous varieties and demonstrate how to incorporate them into a perennial bed and mixed border. We believe this group of clematis is destined to become a mainstay in American gardens.

The Mary Toomey Clematis Garden is an exciting new garden both in design and concept and is surely destined to become a part of any gardener's itinerary when traveling in Northern California.

We hope you will have a chance to visit the garden soon. Simply give us a call at 707-433-8416 to schedule a tour.

of how to keep the garden from being overwhelmed by the incredibly strong and beautiful natural landscape that dominates the view in all directions. It was decided to counter this with an equally strong geometric design, emphasizing circles, squares, and triangles that are used in different ways and with different materials, structures, and plants from garden to garden. Murray suggested that the repetition of

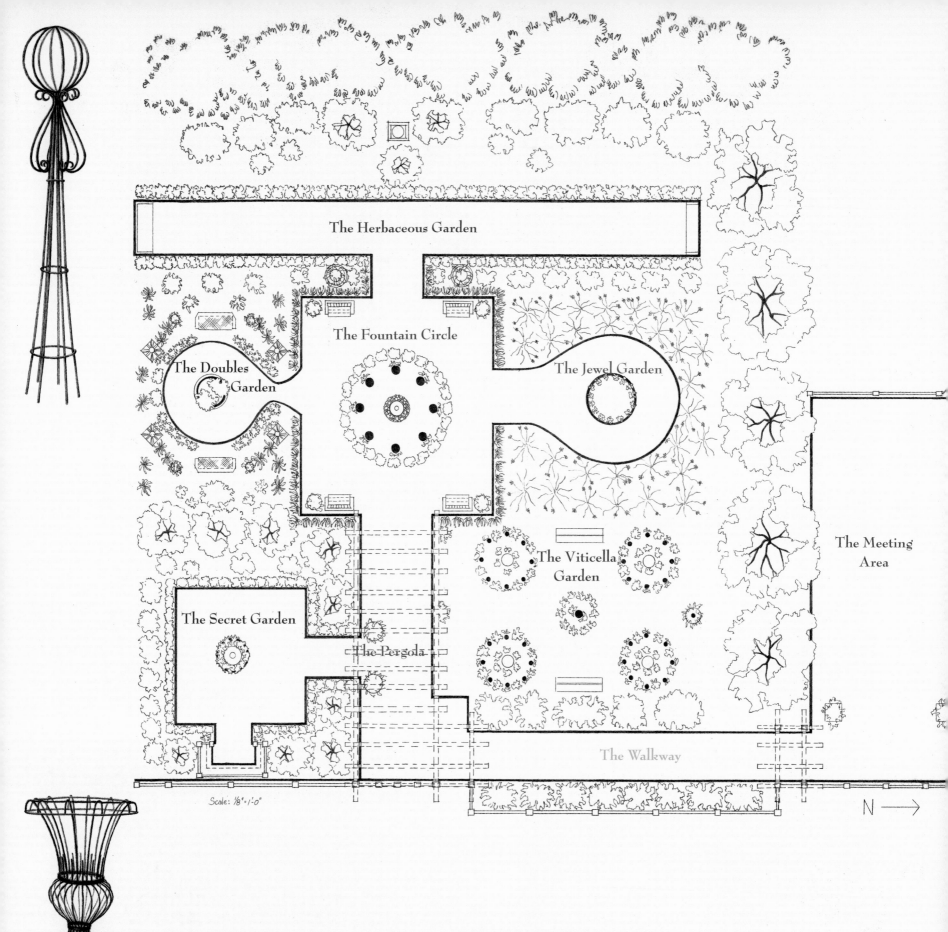

The Herbaceous Garden

The Fountain Circle

The Doubles Garden

The Jewel Garden

The Meeting Area

The Viticella Garden

The Secret Garden

The Pergola

The Walkway

Scale: 1/8" = 1'-0"

N ⟶

The Mary Toomey Garden at Chalk Hill Clematis Nursery

The Mary Toomey Garden Plant List

THE ENTRANCE AND MEETING AREA

Perennials
Geranium sanguineum
Geranium 'Brookside'

Shrubs
Fothergilla 'Mt. Airy'
Hydrangea serrata 'Preziosa'

Trees
Crataegus mollis

Roses
'Eden'
'Danae'
'The Pilgrim'

Vines
C. 'Blekitny Aniol'
C. 'Dominika'
C. 'Huldine'
C. 'Jackmanii'
C. 'Negritianka'
C. 'Polish Spirit'
C. 'Vanessa'
Lonicera japonica 'Aureoreticulata'

THE WALKWAY

Roses
C. 'Cecile Brunner'
'Julia's Rose'

Vines
C. 'Duchess of Albany'
C. 'Francis Rivis'
C. 'Kirigamine'
C. 'Lord Nevill'
C. 'Marie Louise Jensen'
C. 'Markham's Pink'
C. 'Niobe'
C. 'Rouge Cardinal'
C. 'Voluceau'

THE PERGOLA

Perennials
Alchemilla mollis Auslese

Climbing Roses
'Alberic Barbier'
'Butterscotch'
'Compassion'
'Galway Bay'
'Sombrueil'

Vines
C. 'Gravetye Beauty'
C. 'Huldine'
C. 'Lasurstern'
C. 'Marie Boisselot'
C. 'Perle d'Azur'
C. 'Rooguchi'
C. 'Victoria'
C. 'Ville de Lyon'
C. 'Viola'
C. 'Warszawska Nike'

THE VITICELLA GARDEN

Perennials
Eriostemon k. 'Profusion'
Salvia x sylvestris 'May Night'

Shrubs
Philadelphus 'Gallahad'

Vines
C. 'Abundance'
C. 'Alba Luxurians'
C. 'Betty Corning'
C. 'Blue Belle'
C. x diversifolia 'Eriostemon'
C. 'Emilia Platter'
C. 'Étoile Rose'
C. 'Étoile Violette'
C. 'Fairydust'
C. 'Kermesina'
C. 'Little Nell'
C. 'Madame Julia Correvon'
C. 'Minuet'
C. 'M. Koster'
C. 'Mrs. T. Lundell'
C. 'Pagoda'
C. 'Perrin's Pride'
C. 'Venosa Violacea'
C. viticella

THE SECRET GARDEN

Perennials
Convolvulus mauritanicus
Geranium 'Ann Folkard'

Shrubs
Buxus 'Green Velvet'
Philadelphus x virginalis
Viburnum x burkwoodii

Roses
'Abraham Darby'
'Aimee Vibert'
'Graham Thomas'

'Sombrueil'

Vines
'Anita'
'Arabella'
'Étoile Violette'
viorna

THE FOUNTAIN CIRCLE

Shrubs
Buxus 'Green Velvet'
Lavandula 'Hidcote'

Vines
C. 'Allanah'
C. 'Caroline'
C. 'Comtesse de Bouchaud'
C. 'Étoile Rose'
C. 'Prince Charles'

THE JEWEL GARDEN

Perennials
Carex comans 'Bronze'
Gaura lindheimeri 'Whirling Butterflies'

Shrubs
Philadelphus 'Gallahad'

Roses
'Gruss an Aachen'

Vines
C. 'Barbara'
C. 'Ernest Markham'
C. 'Kaeper'
C. 'Kardynal Wyszynski'
C. 'Niobe'
C. 'Sunset'
C. 'Viola'
C. 'Warszawska Nike'

THE DOUBLES GARDEN

Perennials
Agapanthus 'Storm Cloud'
Geranium 'Brookside'
Geranium sanguineum var. striatum

Shrubs
Philadelphus x virginalis

Roses
'Abraham Darby'

'Gruss an Aachen'

Vines
C. 'Arctic Queen'
C. 'Belle of Woking'
C. 'Countess of Lovelace'
C. 'Duchess of Edinburgh'
C. florida var. flore-pleno
C. 'Kiri Te Kanawa'
C. 'Teshio'
C. 'Violet Elizabeth'
C. 'Vyvyan Pennell'

THE HERBACEOUS GARDEN

Perennials
Acanthus mollis
Allium 'Gladiator'
Allium 'Globemaster'
Allium giaganteum 'White giant'
Chrysanthemum parthenium 'Aureum'
Crambe cordifolia
Eupatorium rugosum 'Chocolate'
Euphorbia characias ssp. wulfenii 'Lambrook Gold'
Galega 'Lady Wilson'
Leucanthemum superba 'Becky'
Nepeta x faasenii 'Walker's Low'
Penstemon digitalis 'Huskers Red'

Shrubs
Philadelphus 'Avalanche'

Roses
'Buff Beauty'
'Evelyn'
'Mayor of Casterbridge'
'Mutabilis'

Vines
C. 'Alionushka'
C. x diversifolia 'Olgae'
C. 'Hakuree'
C. integrifolia 'Alba'
C. 'Pamiat Serdtsa'
C. 'Petit Faucon' ('Evisix')
C. 'Paul Farges'
C. recta 'Purpurea'
C. 'Sizaia Ptitsia'
C. tangutica subsp. obtusiuscula 'Gravetye Variety'

The Entrance

mg kemp 2006

mgkemp 2006

THE ATRAGENE GROUP

Includes the alpina, chiisinensis, koreana and macropetala groups. Nodding, lantern or bell-shaped flowers, spring flowering on the growth of the previous year and tolerant of cold temperatures.

'Albiflora' alpina (1955 M. Johnson) Creamy white, bell-shaped flowers with light green staminoides and finely cut light green foliage. Flowers mid-to-late spring.
Height: 6-8 ft. • No Pruning (1)
Zones: 3-9 • Sun / Part shade

'Albiflora'

alpina 'Odorata' alpina (1980 M. Johnson) The mid-blue, bell-shaped flowers are sweetly scented especially if given a sunny aspect. Flowers mid-to-late spring.
Height: 8-10 ft. • No Pruning (1)
Zones: 3-9 • Sun / Part shade

---

alpina 'Pamela Jackman' alpina (1960) Nodding, bell-shaped, deep azure blue flowers with creamy white stamens. Flowers mid-to-late spring.
Height: 8-10 ft. • No Pruning (1)
Zones: 3-9 • Sun / Part shade

'Blue Bird' macropetala (1962 Skinner) Mauve-blue, semi-double, bell-shaped flowers with a lovely inner skirt of pale blue surrounding a central boss of white stamens. Flowers mid-to-late spring.
Height: 8-10 ft. • No Pruning (1)
Zones: 3-9 • Sun / Part shade

'Blue Dancer' alpina (1995) Slender, pale, silver blue, 3-in. bell-

'Blue Bird'

'Blue Dancer'

'Brunette'

'Burford White'

shaped flowers. Flowers in mid-to-late spring.
Height: 6-8 ft. • No Pruning (1)
Zones: 3-9 • Sun / Part shade

'Brunette' Atragene Group (1979 M. Johnson) Bell-shaped flowers of satiny plum-purple. Flowers spring with some re-bloom.
Height: 8-12 ft. • No Pruning (1)
Zones: 3-9 • Sun / Part shade

'Burford White' alpina (c. 1985 Treasures of Tenbury) Creamy white, bell-shaped flowers that show nicely against the light green, finely cut foliage. Flowers mid-to-late spring.
Height: 6-8 ft. • No Pruning (1)
Zones: 3-9 • Sun / Part shade

'Cecile' Atragene Group (Caddick's

'Constance'

'Cecile'

Clematis Nursery) Nodding, bell-shaped, metallic blue flowers with blue staminodes. Flowers spring.
Height: 8-10 ft. • No Pruning (1)
Zones: 3-9 • Sun / Part shade

---

chiisanensis 'Lemon Bells' Atragene Group This selection from South Korea was introduced by the University of British Columbia in 1992. Charming, pale lemon, 2-3-in. long, bell-shaped flowers with a hint of purplish red at the base. Flowers late spring to early summer with some additional blooms later.
Height: 10 ft. • No Pruning (1)
Zones: 6-9 • Sun / Part shade

'Constance' alpina (1992) Deep, reddish-pink, semi-double, nodding, bell-shaped flowers. Free flowering. Flowers mid-to-late spring.
Height: 8-10 ft. • No Pruning (1)

'Foxy'

'Jan Lindmark'

macropetala

'Francis Rivis'

'Jacqueline du Pré'

'Helsingborg'

macropetala 'Lagoon' C.

Zones: 3-9 • Sun / Part shade

___

'Dark Secret' Atagene Group Dark purple outside and powdery purple inside. In the koreana tribe. Flowers spring with some flowers later.
Height: 8 ft. • No Pruning (1)
Zones: 3-9 • Sun / shade

___

'Foxy' alpina (1996 R. Evison) Pale pink, bell-shaped flowers

with a pretty inner skirt of pink staminodes. Flowers mid-to-late spring with some re-bloom later.
Height: 8-10 ft. • No Pruning (1)
Zones: 3-9 • Sun / Part shade

___

'Francesca' Atragene Group (M. Oviatt-Ham) Bell-shaped, pale pink sepals darkening towards the base. Flowers spring.
Height: 8 ft. • No Pruning (1)
Zones: 3-9 • Sun / Part shade

'Frances Rivis' alpina (pre 1965 C. Morris) Bell-shaped flowers with long, tapering sepals of mid-blue. Flowers in mid-to-late spring.
Height: 8-10 ft. • No Pruning (1)
Zones: 3-9 • Sun / Part shade

___

'Frankie' Atragene Group (1991 R. Evison) Nodding, bell-shaped, blue sepals with creamy white staminodes. Flowers spring.
Height: 8-10 ft. • No Pruning (1)
Zones: 3-9 • Sun / Part shade

___

'Helsingborg' alpina (1970) Striking, deep blue-purple, nodding, bell-shaped flowers. A real beauty. Flowers spring.
Height: 8-10 ft. • No Pruning (1)
Zones: 3-9 • Sun / Part shade

___

'Jacqueline du Pré' alpina (1985

B. Fretwell) Named after the late British cellist. Semi-nodding, bell-shaped, pale-pink flowers with slivery-pink edges. Flowers spring.
Height: 8-10 ft. • No Pruning (1)
Zones: 3-9 • Sun / Part shade

___

'Jan Lindmark' macropetala (pre 1981 Lindmark) Purple-mauve with darker streaks and an inner skirt that is paler in color. Flowers early spring.
Height: 6-8 ft. • No Pruning (1)
Zones: 3-9 • Sun / Part shade

___

Koreana var. fragrans Atragene Group (1976) Brownish ruby-red, nodding, bell-shaped and slightly

'Dark Secret'

fragrant. Flowers early spring to early summer.
Height: 10-12 ft. • No Pruning (1)
Zones: 3- 9 • Sun / Part shade

'Lincolnshire Lady' Atragene Group (pre 1992 F. Meechan) Nodding, double, deep, dusky violet-blue. Flowers spring with some repeat bloom.
Height: 8-10 ft. • No Pruning (1)
Zones: 3-9 • Sun / Part shade

'armandii 'Snowdrift'

'Markham's Pink'

---

macropetala (species 1829) Dark lavender-blue, bell-shaped flowers in early spring.
Height: 8-10 ft. • No Pruning (1)
Zones: 3-9 • Sun / Part shade

---

macropetala **'Lagoon'** macropetala (pre 1958 Jackman) Deep blue, nodding, bell-shaped flowers with an inner skirt the same color surrounding a boss of creamy white stamens. Flowers late spring to early summer.
Height: 8-12 ft. • No Pruning (1)
Zones: 3-9 • Sun / Part shade

macropetala **'Maidwell Hall'** macropetala (pre 1956 Jackman) Bell-shaped, deep lavender blue

---

sepals surround inner skirt of similar color with white staminodes. Flowers mid-to-late spring.
Height: 6-8 ft. • No Pruning (1)
Zones: 3-9 • Sun / Part shade

'Markham's Pink' macropetala (pre 1935 E. Markham) A profusion of beautiful, 3-in., pink, double flowers. Still one of the best pink macropetala forms. Flowers spring.
Height: 8-12 ft. • No Pruning (1)
Zones: 3-9 • Sun / Part shade

'Propertius' Atragene Group (1979 M. Johnson) Bell-shaped, pinkish mauve outside with a lighter colored inner skirt. Slightly scented. Flowers spring.
Height: 8 ft. • No Pruning (1)
Zones: 3-9 • Sun / Part shade

'Purple Spider' macropetala (1992 W. Snoeijer) Nodding, double, dark purple sepals with an inner skirt of the same color. Flowers midspring to late spring.
Height: 6-8 ft. • No Pruning (1)
Zones: 3-9 • Sun / Part shade

'White Swan' Atragene Group

'White Swan'

(1961 Dr. F. Skinner) White, fully double, broadly bell-shaped with twisting sepal. Flowers late spring with some re-bloom later.
Height: 6-8 ft. • No pruning
Zones: 3-9 • Sun / Part shade

'Willy' alpina (pre 1971 Zwijnenburg) Pale pink, bell-shaped flowers with darker rose shadings at the base and contrasting greenish cream stamens. Flowers mid-to-late spring.
Height: 8-10 ft. • No Pruning (1)
Zones: 3-9 • Sun / Part shade

THE EVERGREEN GROUP

Includes the armandii, cirhossa and forsteri groups. These plants are only suited for the more temperate regions of the country so please check your zone to make sure the plant is appropriate for your area.

'Apple Blossom' Armandii Group Masses of fragrant, 2-in., saucer shaped flowers, pale pink in bud, opening to white. Long, pointed, leathery dark green foliage. Flowers early spring.
Height: 20 ft. • No pruning (1)
Zones: 6-9 • Sun / Part shade

---

armandii **'Snowdrift'** Armandii Group (1930's G. Jackman) Masses of pure white 2-in. fragrant flowers. Long pointed leathery dark green foliage. Flowers early spring.
Height: 20 ft. • No pruning (1)
Zones: 6-9 • Sun / Part shade

'Early Sensation'

x cartmanii 'Joe' Forsterii Group (1983 H. & M. Taylor) From New Zealand this outstanding cultivar has masses of small, semi-nodding, white flowers flushed with green. The compact growth habit makes this ideal for a container or the alpine garden. Flowers late spring.
Height: 6 ft. • No pruning (1)
Zones: 7-9 • Sun / Part shade

cirrhosa var. balearica Cirrhosa Group (1783) Very attractive, finely cut foliage and 2-in. nodding, creamy yellow bells with red-brown spots on the inside. Winter flowering.
Height: 15-20 ft. • No pruning (1)
Zones: 7-9 • Sun/ Part shade

cirrhosa 'Ourika Valley' Cirrhosa Group (1986 Erskine) From seed collected in the Ourika Valley, Morocco. Nodding, pale yellow bells with creamy anthers. Attractive glossy green foliage. Winter flowering.
Height: 9-12 ft. • No pruning (1)
Zones: 7-9 • Sun / Part shade

cirrhosa 'Wisley Cream' Cirrhosa Group (R. Evison) Nodding, bell-shaped, 1-in. creamy white flowers with glossy green foliage. Winter flowering.
Height: 15 ft. • No pruning (1)
Zones: 7-9 • Sun / Part shade

'Early Sensation' Forsteri Group (G. Hutchins) Pure white, bowl-shaped, scented flowers with greenish yellow stamens. Dark green well-dissected foliage. Flowers early spring.

x cartmanii 'Joe'

Height: 6.5 ft. • No Pruning (1)
Zones: 7-9 • Sun / Part shade

forsteri Forsteri Group (1791) From New Zealand this species has small, semi-nodding, star-shaped, greenish white, fragrant flowers. Blooms April-May.
Height: 6-8 ft. • No pruning (1)
Zones: 8-9 • Sun / Part shade

THE HERBACEOUS AND NON-CLINGING SHRUBS

This charming and diverse group is used to great effect in the perennial border mixed with other perennials, shrubs and roses.

'Alionushka' Integrifolia Group (1961 Volosenko-Valenis) Rich,

mauve-pink, 3-in. nodding, broadly bell-shaped flowers displayed on a strong growing plant that will need support. Flowers summer to autumn.
Height: 5-7 ft. • Prune hard (3)
Zones: 4-9 • Sun / Part shade

'Anastasiia Anisimova' Integrifolia Group (1958 Volosenko-Valenis) Pale blue, somewhat gappy with wavy margins and yellow anthers. Flowers early summer to autumn.
Height: 4-6 ft. • Prune hard (3)
Zones: 4-9 • Sun / Part shade

'Arabella' Integrifolia Group (1990 B.Fretwell) Lovely, sky blue, open, 2-in. flowers grace this plant. Flowers summer to autumn.
Height: 5-6 ft. • Prune hard (3)
Zones: 4-9 • Sun / Part shade

'Alionushka'

'Arabella'

x Aromatica

x aromatica Herbaceous Group
(1845) Small, fragrant, deep
violet-blue flowers with prominent
yellow stamens. Flowers summer to
autumn.
Height: 6 ft. • Prune hard (3)
Zones: 4-9 • Sun / Part shade

---

x diversifolia 'Blue Boy' Integrifolia
Group (1947 F. Skinner) Bell-
shaped, nodding, 2-3-in. silvery,
mid-blue flowers. Flowers summer
to autumn.
Height: 5-6 ft. • Prune hard (3)
Zones: 4-9 • Sun / Part shade

'Diversifolia Coerulea' Integrifolia
Group (B. Freres) Deep blue, bell-
shaped. Flowers early summer to
late summer.
Height: 2-3 ft. • Prune hard (3)
Zones: 4-9 • Sun / Part shade

---

x diversifolia 'Eriostemon'
Integrifolia Group (c. 1830)
Nodding, bell-shaped, dark purple-
blue with pale yellow anthers.
Flowers early summer to late
summer.
Height: 6-8 ft. • Prune hard (3)
Zones: 4-9 • Sun / Part shade

---

x diversifolia 'Heather Herschell'
Integrifolia Group (1990's B.
Fretwell) Soft pink, bell-shaped
flowers displayed on a vigorous
upright plant that needs support.
Flowers early summer to late
summer.
Height: 6-8 ft. • Prune hard (3)
Zones: 4-9 • Sun / Part shade

x diversifolia 'Eriostemon'

x diversifolia 'Hendryetta'
Integrifolia Group (2003 W.
Snoeijer) Nodding, broadly bell-
shaped, deep rose-pink flowers with
cream colored anthers. Flowers early
to late summer.
Height: 3-4 ft. • Prune hard (3)
Zones: 4-9 • Sun / Part shade

---

x diversifolia 'Olgae' Integrifolia
Group Clear mid-blue, 2-3-in.,
nodding flowers with distinctive
twisted sepals. Sweetly scented.
Flowers early to late summer.
Height: 2 ft. • Prune hard (3)
Zones: 3-9 • Sun / Part shade

---

x durandii Integrifolia Group
(1870 Durand) Deep indigo-blue,
4-in. semi-nodding flowers. An
older variety but still unsurpassed.
Flowers summer to autumn.
Height: 4-6 ft. • Prune hard (3)
Zones: 4-9 • Sun /Part shade

'Edward Prichard' Herbaceous
Group (pre 1950 R. V. Prichard)

x diversifolia 'Olgae'

x durandii

Masses of small, scented, pale
mauve flowers are carried on erect
stems of this herbaceous non-
clinging plant. Flowers mid-to-late
summer.
Height: 3-5 ft. • Prune hard (3)
Zones: 4-9 • Sun / Part shade

'Floris V' Integrifolia Group (1995

H.Vermeulen) Urn shaped flowers of
burgundy red.
Flowers early to late summer.
Height: 3 ft. • Prune hard (3)
Zones: 4-9 • Sun / Part shade

'Hakuree' Integrifolia Group
(K.Ozawa) White, nodding, bell-
shaped flowers with long narrow

twisted sepals. Jasmine scented. Early flowers may be tinged with pale lavender. Flowers early to late summer.
Height: 2-3 ft. • *Prune hard (3)*
Zones: 4-9 • *Sun / Part shade*

'Hendersonii' Integrifolia Group
Nodding, bell-shaped, dusky indigo blue, with long pointed, twisting sepals and yellow anthers. Flowers early summer to late summer.
Height: 2-3 ft. • *Prune hard (3)*
Zones: 3-9 • *Sun / Part shade*

---

heracleifolia 'Cassandra' Heracleifolia Group A semi-upright or scrambling plant that produces

integrifolia 'Alba'

'Pamiat Serdtsa'

small, scented, deep gentian blue, hyacinth-like flowers. Blooms midsummer to autumn.
Height: 3 ft. • *Prune hard (3)*
Zones: 5-9 • *Sun / Part shade*

'Inspiration'('Zoin') Integrifolia Group (2000 W. Snoeijer) Deep pink, 3-in. outward facing flowers. Flowers early to late summer.
Height: 4-6 ft. • *Prune hard (3)*
Zones: 4-9 • *Sun / Part shade*

---

integrifolia Integrifolia Group (1573) Deep blue, 1-in. nodding, bell-like flowers. Flowers early to late summer.
Height: 2-3 ft. • *Prune hard (3)*
Zones: 3-9 • *Sun / Part shade*

---

integrifolia 'Alba' Integrifolia Group
Nodding, bell-shaped, scented, white flowers with yellow anthers. Flowers early to late summer.
Height: 2 ft. • *Prune hard (3)*
Zones: 4-9 • *Sun / Part shade*

integrifolia 'Ozawa's Blue'

integrifolia

Integrifolia Group (K. Ozawa) Nodding, scented, mid-blue to dark blue. Flowers early summer to autumn.
Height: 2-3 ft. • *Prune hard (3)*
Zones: 4-9 • *Sun / Part shade*

'Juuli' Integrifolia Group (1984 Kivistik) Similar to Arabella in habit but with flowers of purple-blue. Flowers early to late summer.
Height: 4-5 ft. • *Prune hard (3)*
Zones: 3-9 • *Sun / Part shade*

'Mrs. Robert Brydon' Heracleifolia Group (1935 R. Brydon) A scrambling, non-clinging, herbaceous clematis that produces masses of small white flowers with a sky-blue margin that curl back to reveal a prominent boss of creamy white anthers. Useful as a ground cover, spilling over a wall or under planting around a tree. Flowers midsummer to autumn.
Height: 8-10 ft. • *Prune hard (3)*
Zones: 3-9 • *Sun / Part shade*

'Pamiat Serdtsa' Integrifolia Group

'Hakuree'

'Pangourne Pink'

(1967 Beskaravainaya) The name translates as "Memory of the Heart." Slightly nodding, broadly bell-shaped, 3-in. flowers of lilac-purple with a satiny sheen. Pale yellow anthers. Flowers early summer to early autumn.
Height: 4-6 ft. • *Prune hard (3)*
Zones: 3-9 • *Sun / Part shade*

'Pangourne Pink' Integrifolia Group (1992 Busheyfields Nursery) Deep pink, nodding, broadly bell-shaped flowers with pale yellow anthers. Lightly scented. Flowers late spring to early autumn.
Height: 2-3 ft. • *Prune hard (3)*
Zones: 3-9 • *Sun / Part shade*

'Pastel Pink' Integrifolia Group (1986 B. Fretwell) Nodding, scented, pale pink, bell-shaped, with sepals recurving and twisting as they

open. Flowers early summer to late summer.

Height: 2-3 ft. • Prune hard (3)
Zones: 3-9 • Sun / Part shade

'Petit Faucon' ('Evisix') Integrifolia Group (1989 R. Evison) A stunning plant with deep violet-blue, shiny, 2-in. flowers and contrasting yellow stamens. As the flower opens the sepals twist in a most interesting way. Flowers early to late summer.

Height: 3 ft. • Prune hard (3)
Zones: 4-9 • Sun / Part shade

recta Flammula Group (1597) Masses of star-shaped, hawthorn-scented, white flowers followed by a nice display of seedheads. Flowers early summer.

Height: 4-6 ft. • Prune hard (3)
Zones: 3-9 • Sun / Part shade

recta 'Purpurea' Flammula Group The young foliage is deep purple maturing to a dark bluish green. Masses of star-shaped, hawthorn-scented, white flowers followed by a nice display of seedheads. Flowers early summer.

Height: 4-6 ft. • Prune hard (3)
Zones: 3-9 • Sun / Part shade

recta 'Velvet Night' Flammula Group (c.1995) Darker purple foliage that lasts longer than its parent 'Purpurea'. Masses of starry-shaped, sweetly scented, white flowers followed by a long lasting display of seedheads. Flowers early summer.

'Petit Faucon'

tubulosa 'Wyvale'

Height: 4-6 ft. • Prune hard (3)
Zones: 3-9 • Sun / Part shade

'Rooguchi' Integrifolia Group (1988 K. Ozawa) Dark plum, 3-in. long, bell-shaped with slightly recurved sepals. Can be prone to mildew. Flowers early summer to autumn.

Height: 6-9 ft. • Prune hard (3)
Zones: 3-9 • Sun / Part shade

Sizaia Ptitsia Integrifolia Group (1979 Beskaravainaya) Violet-purple with light purple anthers. The sepals open wide and twist to nice effect. Flowers early summer to autumn.

Height: 4-6 ft. • Prune hard (3)
Zones: 3-9 • Sun / Part shade

'Tapestry' Integrifolia Group (pre 1989 B. Fretwell) Nodding, bell-

'Rooguchi'

Sizaia Ptitsia

shaped with darker mauve-red tones on the outside and paler mauve-pink on the inside. Flowers early summer to late summer.

Height: 2-3 ft. • Prune hard (3)
Zones: 3-9 • Sun / Part shade

tubulosa (Syn. davidiana) Heracleifolia Group (1863) Tubular, hyacinth-like, scented, powder-blue flowers. Blooms early summer to late summer..

Height: 3 ft. • Prune hard (3)
Zones: 3-9 • Sun / Part shade

tubulosa 'Wyevale' Heracleifolia

Group (ca. 1955 H. Williamson) Strongly scented, tubular, hyacinth-like, deep mid-blue flowers. The sepals reflex back showing off the yellow stamens. Flowers midsummer to early autumn.
Height: 3-4 ft. • Prune hard (3)
Zones: 3-9 • Sun / Part shad

THE LARGE FLOWERED HYBRIDS

The Early Large-flowered Group bloom in late spring-early summer on wood ripened from the previous season. A light pruning after the first period of flowering will encourage another round of flowering later in the summer to early autumn. The Late Large-flowered Group produce their flowers from early to midsummer to Autumn. Varieties in this are group pruned hard in late winter to early spring, producing flowers on the new growth.

'Alabast'

'Andromeda'

'Akaisha' Early Large-flowered Group (1996 Sakata no Tane Co.) Deep, violet-blue, boat-shaped sepals with a deep carmine bar and purple red anthers. Flowers in late spring to early summer and late summer.
Height: 8-10 ft. • Prune light (2)
Zones 4-9 • Sun / Part shade

'Alabast' *('Poulala')* Early Large-flowered Group (D.T. Poulsen 1970) Large creamy white flowers with yellow stamens, tinged green in cooler late spring temperatures or part shade. Flowers late spring to early summer and late summer.
Height: 10 ft. • Prune light (2)
Zones: 4-9 • Sun / Part shade

'Alice Fisk' Early Large-flowered Group (1964 J. Fisk) Pale wisterias-blue, long pointed sepals, slightly wavy margins and dark brown anthers. Flowers late spring

'Arctic Queen'

'Asao'

'Allanah'

to early summer and late summer.
Height: 6-8 ft. • Prune light (2)
Zones: 4-9 • Sun / Part shade

'Allanah' Late Large-flowered Group (1968 A. Keay) Large velvety, deep ruby-red flowers with almost black anthers. Flowers summer to autumn.
Height: 8 ft. • Prune hard (3)
Zones: 3-9 • Sun

'Andromeda' Early Large-flowered Group (Pyne 1987) White flowers with a dramatic splash of raspberry along the mid rib from the base. First blooms semi double and single later. Flowers late spring to early summer and late summer.
Height: 10 ft. • Prune light (2)
Zones: 4-9 • Sun / Part shade

'Ania' Early Large-flowered Group

(1980 Franczak) Lovely soft pink with yellow anthers. Flowers late spring to early summer and late summer.
Height: 6-8 ft. • Prune light (2)
Zones: 4-9 • Sun / Part shade

'Anna Louise' *('Evithree')* Early Large-flowered Group (1993 R. Evison) Vivid violet-blue with a red-purple bar and deep red anthers. Flowers late spring to early summer and late summer.
Height: 6-8 ft. • Prune light (2)
Zones: 4-9 • Sun / Part shade

'Aotearoa' Late Large-flowered Group (1992 A. Keay) Violet-purple with creamy green stamens. Flowers midsummer to autumm.
Height: 12 ft. • Prune hard (3)
Zones: 4-9 • Sun

'**Arctic Queen**' ('*Evitwo*') Early Large-flowered Group (1994 R. Evison) Pure white, double rosette-shaped flowers with creamy white anthers. Double flowers on old and new wood. Flowers early summer to autumn.
Height: 9-12 ft. • Prune light (2)
Zones: 4-9 • Sun / Part shade

'**Asao**' Early Large-flowered Group (1971 K. Ozawa) Deeper pink at the margins and a pale pink almost white bar. Bright golden anthers. Flowers late spring to early summer and late summer to autumn.
Height: 8-10 ft. • Prune light (2)
Zones: 4-9 • Sun / Part shade

'**Ascotiensis**' Late Large-flowered Group (1871) Deep mid-blue flowers with greenish brown anthers. A fine old variety often grown with roses. Flowers midsummer to autumn.
Height: 10-12 ft. • Prune hard (3)
Zones: 3-9 • Sun / Part shade

'**Bagatelle**' (*Syn.* '*Dorothy Walton*') Late Large-flowered Group (Pre 1930) Star-like, silvery, mauve pink with pale reddish brown stamens. Flowers midsummer to autumn.
Height: 10-12 ft. • Prune hard (3)
Zones: 4-9 • Sun / Part shade

'**Baltyk**' Early Large-flowered Group (1970 Franczak) Purple-violet with faint reddish purple bar, cream colored filaments and crimson anthers. Flowers late spring to early summer and late summer.
Height: 6 ft. • Prune light (2)
Zones: 4-9 • Sun / Part shade

'**Barbara**' Late Large-flowered Group (1993 Marczynski) Vivid, purple pink with dark purple anthers. Flowers midsummer to autumn.
Height: 9 ft. • Prune hard (3)
Zones: 4-9 • Sun / Part shade

'**Barbara Harrington**' Late Large-flowered Group (1996 D. Harrington) Red-purple flowers with slightly wavy margins and yellow anthers. A sport of the very popular 'Comtesse de Bouchaud'. Flowers midsummer to autumn.
Height: 10-12 ft. • Prune hard (3)
Zones: 4-9 • Sun

'**Barbara Jackman**' Early Large-flowered Group (1952 Jackman) Mauve-blue with a crimson red bar and contrasting creamy yellow stamens. Flowers late spring to early summer and late summer.
Height: 6-8 ft. • Prune light (2)
Zones: 4-9 • Sun / Part shade

'**Beauty of Worcester**' Early Large-flowered Group (pre 1886 R. Smith & Co.) Blooms semi-double and double on wood of the previous season and single on current year's growth. Complex colors of deep reddish purple outer sepals and hints of violet, blue, and pink on the inner sepals complemented by creamy yellow stamens. Late spring to early summer and late summer.
Height: 6-8 ft. • Prune light (2)
Zones: 4-9 • Sun / Part shade

'**Bees Jubilee**' Early Large-flowered Group (pre 1958 Bees' Nursery)

'Bagatelle'

'Baltyk'

'Barbara'

'Belle Nantaise'

Light, mauve-pink with a deeper pink bar. Best in part shade. Flowers late spring to early summer and late summer to early autumn.
Height: 6-8 ft. • Prune Light (2)
Zones: 4-9 • Sun / Part shade

'Bella' Early Large-flowered Group (1982 Kivistik) White with a cream bar and dark red anthers. Flowers late spring to early summer and late summer to autumn.
Height: 6-8 ft. • Prune light (2)
Zones: 4-9 • Sun/ Part shade

'Belle Nantaise' Early Large-flowered Group (1887 Boisselot) Pure lavender-blue with prominent creamy yellow stamens. Flowers late spring to early summer and late summer to autumn.
Height: 10 ft. • Prune light (2)
Zones: 4-9 • Sun / Part shade

'Belle of Woking' Early Large-flowered Group (pre 1881 Jackman) Rosette-shaped, always double, silvery mauve flowers. Flowers early summer to late summer.
Height: 6-8 ft. • Prune light (2)
Zones: 4-9 • Sun / Part shade

'Blekitny Aniol'

'Black Tea' Late Large-flowered Group (1995 H. Hayakawa) Dark, velvety, purple-red with a dark red bar and reddish brown anthers. Flowers early summer to early autumn.
Height: 8 ft. • Prune hard (3)
Zones: 4-9 • Sun / Part shade

'Blekitny Aniol' ('Blue Angel') Late Large-flowered Group (1987 S. Franczak) Masses of mid-sized pastel sky blue flowers with greenish-yellow stamens. Flowers early summer to autumn.
Height: 10-12 ft. • Prune hard (3)
Zones: 4-9 • Sun / Part shade

'Blue Eyes' Early Large-flowered Group (1987 K. Pyne) Sky-blue with yellow anthers. Flowers late spring to early summer and late summer.
Height: 6-8 ft. • Prune light (2)
Zones: 4-9 • Sun / Part shade

'Blue Gem' Early Large-flowered Group (1875 Jackman) Satiny, sky blue, fading to mauve with red-purple anthers. Flowers late spring

'Belle of Woking'

'Blue Light'

to early summer and late summer to autumn.
Height: 10-12 ft. • Prune light (2)
Zones: 4-9 • Sun / Part shade

'Blue Light' ('Vanso') Early Large-flowered Group (1998 F. van Haastert) Pale-blue, double flowers in late spring to early summer and both single and double flowers later in the summer. Flowers late spring

to early summer and late summer to autumn.
Height: 8 ft. • Prune light (2)
Zones: 4-9 • Sun / Part shade

'**Blue Ravine**' Early Large-flowered Group (1978 C. Erlandson) Intriguing mauve-blue with deeper mauve midribs and contrasting purple and white stamens. Strong grower and well suited to the hot North American summers. Flowers late spring to early summer and late summer to autumn.
Height: 8-10 ft. • Prune light (2)
Zones: 4-9 • Sun / Part shade

'**Candida**' Early Large-flowered Group (1862 Lemoine) Elegant, pure white flowers with cream stamens. Flowers late spring to early summer and late summer to early autumn.
Height: 10 ft. • Prune light (2)
Zones: 4-9 • Sun / Part shade

'**Carnaby**' Early Large-flowered Group (1983 Treasures) Raspberry pink with a darker pink bar and red anthers. Flowers late spring to early summer and late summer to autumn.
Height: 6-8 ft. • Prune light (2)

'Carnival'

Zones: 4-9 • Sun / Part shade

'**Carnival**' Early Large-flowered Group (1989 Spring Valley Greenhouse Inc.) Powder blue with a deep lavender bar and bright yellow stamens. Flowers late spring to early summer and late summer to autumn.
Height: 6-8 ft. • Prune light (2)
Zones: 4-9 • Sun / Part shade

'**Caroline**' Late Large-flowered Group (1990 B. Fretwell) Delicate shades of light pink and peach with a darker central bar make this well formed flower with pointed sepals a most interesting variety. Best in part shade. Flowers early summer to early autumn.
Height: 6-8 ft. • Prune hard (3)
Zones: 4-9 • Sun / Part shade

'Blue Ravine'

'Charissima'

'**Chalcedony**' Early Large-flowered Group (1984 E. Strachan) Double flowers of pale silvery-blue or pale pink and green tones depending on weather and soil conditions. Creamy yellow stamens. Flowers late spring to early summer and late summer.
Height: 8-10 ft. • Prune light (2)
Zones: 4-9 • Sun / Part shade

'**Charissima**' Early Large-flowered Group (1974 W. Pennell) Very showy flower of cerise pink, slightly deeper pink bar and veining with maroon anthers. Flowers late spring to early summer and late summer.
Height: 8-10 ft. • Prune light (2)
Zones: 4-9 • Sun / Part shade

'**Claire de Lune**' ('**Evirin**') Early Large-flowered Group (1997 R. Evison) Wavy edged sepals of white, suffused with pale lilac. Nicely contrasting red anthers. Part shade

'Claire de Lune'

is best. Flowers late spring to early summer and late summer to early autumn.
Height: 8-10 ft. • Prune light (2)
Zones: 4-9 • Sun / Part shade

'**Colette Deville**' Early Large-flowered Group (1985 A. Leroy) Early flowers are deep red-purple with a light mauve bar and red anthers. Later flowers are solid red-purple. A treasure from the past. Flowers late spring to early summer and late summer.
Height: 10 ft. • Prune light (2)
Zones: 4-9 • Sun / Part shade

'**Comtesse de Bouchaud**' Late Large-flowered Group (pre 1900 F. Morel) Beautiful 4-5-in. mid-pink flowers with creamy yellow anthers. Flowers midsummer to autumn.
Height: 10 ft. • Prune hard (3)
Zones: 4-9 • Sun / Part shade

'Countess of Lovelace' Early Large-flowered Group (1871 Jackman) Double flowers of lavender blue with yellow anthers on previous year's wood followed by single flowers later on new growth. Flowers late spring to early summer and late summer.
Height: 6-8 ft. • Prune light (2)
Zones: 4-9 • Sun / Part shade

'Crimson King' Late Large-flowered Group (A.G. Jackman 1915) Dark carmine red flowers with purplish brown anthers. Flowers summer to

'Dawn'

autumn.
Height: 8-10 ft. • Prune hard (2)
Zones: 4-9 • Sun / Part shade

'Crystal Fountain' ('Fairy Blue') Early Large-flowered Group (1994 Hayakawa) Double flowers of lilac blue with a very showy, pronounced center of creamy yellow stamens. Flowers late spring to early summer and late summer.
Height: 4-6 ft. • Prune hard (2)
Zones: 4-9 • Sun / Part shade

'C.W. Dowman' Early Large-

'Dominika'

flowered Group (W. Pennell 1953) Delicate pale pink with a deeper pink central bar. Part shade is best. Flowers early summer to late summer.
Height: 8-10 ft. • Prune light (2)
Zones: 4-9 • Sun / Part shade

'Daniel Deronda' Early Large-flowered Group (pre 1882 C. Noble). Very large deep purple-blue flowers with creamy yellow anthers. Early flowers are sometimes semi-double. Also produces exceptional attractive seed heads. Named after the last book written by George Eliot. Flowers late spring to early summer and late summer.
Height: 6-8 ft. • Prune light (2)
Zones: 4-9 • Sun / Part shade

'Dawn' Early Large-flowered Group (c.1960 T. Lundell) Lovely pearly-pink tepals and prominent purple anthers. Partial shade will enhance

the delicate color. Flowers late spring to early summer and late summer.
Height: 6-8 ft. • Prune light (2)
Zones: 4-9 • Sun / Part shade

'Denny's Double' Early Large-flowered Group (1977 V. Denny) Nicely formed double flowers of lilac-mauve fading to light blue. Flowers late spring to early summer and late summer.
Height: 10 ft. • Prune light (2)
Zones: 4-9 • Sun / Part shade

'Doctor Ruppel' Early Large-flowered Group (pre 1975 Ruppel) Brilliant rose pink with a deeper central bar. Light brown stamens. Flowers late spring to early summer and late summer to autumn.
Height: 10 ft. • Prune light (2)
Zones: 4-9 • Sun / Part shade

'C.W. Dowman'

'Dorota'

'Dominika' Late Large-flowered Group (1972 S. Franczak) Pale mauve-blue, strong mauve veining, edged in a darker mauve with greenish yellow anthers. Flowers summer to autumn.
Height: 8-10 ft. • Prune hard (3)
Zones: 4-9 • Sun / Part shade

'Dorota' Early Large-flowered Group (1978 S. Franczak) Deep violet-blue, wavy margins and lilac anthers. Flowers early summer and late summer to autumn.
Height: 9 ft. • Prune light (2)
Zones: 4-9 • Sun / Part shade

'Dorothy Tolver' Early Large-flowered Group (1987 J. Gooch) Overlapping sepals of deep mauve pink with a textured satiny surface. Flowers late spring to early summer and late summer to autumn.
Height: 8-12 ft. • Prune light (2)
Zones: 4-9 • Sun / Part shade

'Duchess of Edinburgh' Early Large-flowered Group (pre 1874 G. Jackman & Son) Extraordinary double, 4-6-in. white flowers that exhibit green overtones in partial shade or cool spring temperatures. The flowers in the second flowering period are somewhat smaller. Flowers late spring through early summer and late summer.
Height: 6-8 ft. • Prune light (2)
Zones: 4-9 • Sun / Part shade

'Edith' Early Large-flowered Group (pre 1974 R. Evison) Attractive white flowers with dark red anthers.

'Duchess of Edinburgh'

Flowers exhibit a green bar in first bloom period. Flowers late spring to early summer and late summer.
Height: 6-8 ft. • Prune light (2)
Zones: 4-9 • Sun / Part shade

'Edomurasaki' Early Large-flowered Group (1952 S. Arai) Regal, deep velvety purple with deep red anthers. Flowers late spring to early summer and late summer to autumn.
Height: 8-10 ft. • Prune light (2)
Zones: 4-9 • Sun / Part shade

'Édouard Desfossé' Early Large-flowered Group (pre 1880 Desfosse) Pale blue flowers with a satiny sheen and blue-mauve mid ribs. Flowers late spring to early summer and late summer.
Height: 4-6 ft. • Prune light (2)
Zones: 4-9 • Sun / Part shade

'Ekstra' Late Large-flowered Group (1982 Kivistik) Light blue-violet with a paler violet-blue bar and dark

'Edomurasaki'

Édouard Desfossé

violet anthers. Flowers midsummer to autumn.
Height: 6-8 ft. • Prune hard (3)
Zones: 4-9 • Sun / Part shade

'Elsa Späth' Early Large-flowered Group (1891 Spath) Violet-blue with deep red anthers. Strong growing and free flowering. Flowers

'Elsa Späth'

'Fireworks'

florida var. flore-pleno

'Fryderyk Chopin'

'Frau Mikiko'

late spring to early summer and late summer to autumn.
Height: 10 ft. • Prune light (2)
Zones: 4-9 • Sun / Part shade

'Ernest Markham' Late Large-flowered Group (1926 E. Markham) Velvety, magenta red with pale yellow brown anthers. Best in full sun. Flowers early summer to autumn.
Height: 10-12 ft. • Prune hard (3)
Zones: 4-9 • Sun

'Fair Rosamond' Early Large-Flowered Group (1871 G. Jackman) Blush white with a pale pink bar and deep red stamens. Scented. Part shade is best. Flowers late spring to early summer and late summer.
Height: 8 ft. • Prune light (2)
Zones: 4-9 • Sun / Part shade

'Fireworks' (1980 J. Treasure) Purple-blue with a purple-red bar and red anthers. Flowers late spring to early summer and late summer .
Height: 8-10 ft. • Prune light (2)
Zones: 4-9 • Sun / Part shade

---

florida var. *flore-pleno* (Syn. *florida* 'Plena') Late Large-flowered Group (c.1835) Greenish white, double, 4-in. rosette-shaped flowers. Flowers summer to early autumn.
Height: 6-8 ft. • Prune hard (3)
Zones: 7-9 • Sun / Part shade

---

florida var. *sieboldiana* (Syn. *florida* 'Sieboldiana') Late Large-flowered Group (1836 von Siebold) Creamy white tepals surround a prominent mass of purple stamens, creating

a very regal looking 4-in. flower. Flowers summer to autumn.
Height: 6-8 ft. • Prune hard (3)
Zones: 7-9 • Sun / Part shade

'Frau Mikiko' Early Large-flowered Group (1993 K. Sugimoto) Intense violet-blue with a reddish bar towards the base, wavy margins and yellow anthers. A real beauty. Flowers late spring to early summer and late summer to late autumn.
Height: 8-10 ft. • Prune light (2)
Zones: 4-9 • Sun / Part shade

'Fryderyk Chopin' Early Large-flowered Group (pre 1994 S. Franczak) Clear metalic blue with wavy edged sepals and creamy colored stamens. Best in part shade. Flowers early summer to late summer.
Height: 6-8 ft. • Prune light (2)
Zones: 4-9 • Sun / Part shade

'Fujimusume' Early Large-flowered Group (1952 S. Arai) An outstanding cultivar from Japan. Sky-blue flowers with yellow

florida var. sieboldiana

'Fujimusume'

'General Sikorski'

anthers. Flowers early and late summer.
Height: 8-10 ft. • Prune light (2)
Zones: 4-9 • Sun / Part shade

'General Sikorski' Early Large-flowered Group (W. Noll) Mauve-blue flowers with golden yellow anthers. Vigorous and free flowering. Flowers late spring to early autumn.
Height: 10 ft. • Prune light (2)
Zones: 4-9 • Sun / Part shade

'Gillian Blades' Early Large-flowered Group (1975 J. Fisk) White flowers with distinctly ruffled edges. In cool weather or part shade the margins of each sepal can take on a lavender tone. Flowers late spring to early summer and late summer.
Height: 6-8 ft. • Prune light (2)
Zones: 4-9 • Sun / Part shade

'Gillian Blades'

'Gipsy Queen' Late Large-flowered Group (1877 T. Cripps) Large, velvety, dark plum purple flowers with red anthers. Flowers summer to early autumn.
Height: 10-12 ft. • Prune hard (3)
Zones: 3-9 • Sun / Part shade

'Gladys Picard' Early Large-flowered Group (1972 J. Fisk) Pale mauve-pink flowers, wavy margins and pale yellow anthers. Flowers late spring to early summer and late summer.
Height: 8-10 ft. • Prune light (2)
Zones: 3-9 • Sun / Part shade

'Guernsey Cream' Early Large-flowered Group (1989 R. Evison) Creamy white rounded sepals with yellow anthers. Flowers late spring to early summer and late summer.
Height: 6-8 ft. • Prune light (2)
Zones: 4-9 • Sun / Part shade

'Hagley Hybrid' Late Large-flowered Group (1945 P. Picton) The shell pink with dark red anthers. Partial shade is best. Flowers early summer to late summer.
Height: 8 ft. • Prune hard (3)

'Gipsy Queen'

Zones: 4-9 • Sun / Part shade

'Hakuba' Early Large-flowered Group (1973 H. Hayakawa) Delicate, pale lilac with creamy yellow anthers. Flowers in late spring to early summer and late

'Hagley Hybrid'

'Hakuba'

summer.
Height: 8-10 ft. • Prune light (2)
Zones: 4-9 • Sun / Part shade

'Hakuookan' Early Large-flowered Group (pre 1957 Kubota) Deep violet-blue with very prominent

'Hakuookan'

'H.F. Young'

'Hania'

white stamens. Flowers late spring to early summer and early autumn.
Height: 6-8 ft. • Prune light (2)
Zones: 4-9 • Sun / Part shade

'Halina Noll' Early Large-flowered Group (1974 W. Noll) White flowers tinged with pale purple/pink and with yellow anthers. Early flowers are sometimes double. Flowers late spring to early summer and late summer.
Height: 8-10 ft. • Prune light (2)
Zones: 4-9 • Sun / Part shade

'Hania' Early Large-flowered Group (1993 Marczynski) Velvety, deep purplish red with deeper reddish purple on the margins and yellow anthers. Flowers late spring to early summer and late summer to autumn.
Height: 6 ft. • Prune light (2)
Zones: 4-9 • Sun / Part shade

'Henryi' Early Large-flowered Group (1855 Anderson-Henry) White flowers with contrasting dark maroon stamens. In a shaded aspect or cool weather a green stripe will show on each sepal. Flowers late spring to early summer and late summer to autumn.
Height: 10-12 ft. • Prune light (2)
Zones: 4-9 • Sun / Part shade

'H.F. Young' Early Large-flowered Group (W. Pennell 1954) Deep lavender blue flowers with creamy white stamens. Flowers late spring to early summer and late summer.
Height: 6-8 ft. • Prune light (2)
Zones: 4-9 • Sun / Part shade

'Honora' Late Large-flowered Group (Mrs. A. Edwards) Long, tapered sepals of rich, violet-purple, shaded with burgundy and deep, purple-red anthers. The slightly crimped margins add to an already stunning flower. Flowers summer to autumn.
Height: 10-12 ft. • Prune hard (3)
Zones: 4-9 • Sun / Part shade

'Huldine' Late Large-flowered Group (pre 1914 Morel) Strong grower with 3-in. pearly white flowers and pale mauve reverse.

'Huldine'

'Henryi'

'Isago'

'Jan Pawel 11'

Flowers early summer to late summer.
Height: 15-20 ft. • Prune hard (3)
Zones: 4-9 • Sun

'Ice Blue' ('Evipoo3') Early Large-flowered Group (2005 Evison/Paulsen) White flowers washed in a cool blue with creamy white anthers. Flowers late spring to early summer and late summer.
Height: 6-8 ft. • Prune light (2)
Zone 4-9 • Sun / Part shade

'Isago' Early Large-flowered Group (1991 S. Arafume) Double, pure white flowers with yellow anthers, semi-double later. Flowers late spring to early summer and late summer.
Height: 6-8 ft. • Prune light (2)
Zones: 4-9 • Sun / Part shade

'Ivan Olsson' Early Large-flowered Group (1955 M. Johnson) Pale ice blue flowers with slightly darker margins. Flowers late spring to early summer and late summer.
Height: 6-8 ft. • Prune light (2)
Zones: 4-9 • Sun / Part shade

'Jackmanii' Late Large-flowered Group (1858 Jackman) Velvety, deep royal purple flowers with creamy green anthers. Flowers early summer to autumn.
Height: 10-12 ft. • Prune hard (3)
Zones: 3-9 • Sun / Part shade

'Jackmanii Alba' Early Large-flowered Group (Noble 1878) Double and semi-double white flowers on previous year's wood and single flowers on new growth. Flowers late spring to early summer

and late summer.
Height: 10-12 ft. • Prune light (2)
Zones: 4-9 • Sun / Part shade

'Jackmanii Superba' Late Large-flowered Group (c.1880 T. Cripps) Deep plum-purple with red shading along the midrib that fades as the flower matures. The sepals are a little broader than Jackmanii. Flowers early to late summer.
Height: 10-12 ft. • Prune hard (3)
Zones: 3-9 • Sun / Part shade

'Jan Pawel II' Early Large-flowered Group (1966 S. Franczak) Creamy white with a hint of pink, a light pink bar on both sides and dark purple-red anthers. Flowers early summer to late summer.
Height: 8-10 ft. • Prune light (2)
Zones: 4-9 • Sun / Part shade

'John Warren' Early Large-flowered Group (1968 W. Pennell) Large flowers of lilac pink cast over grayish white with stronger central bar, veining, and margins. Purple red anthers. Flowers late spring to early summer and late summer.
Height: 8-10 ft. • Prune light (2)
Zones: 4-9 • Sun / Part shade

'Josephine' ('Evijohill') Early Large-flowering Group (1980 Mrs. J. Hill) Large double rosette flowers of lilac-pink with a deeper pink bar. The inner sepals are sometimes tinged with green. Flowers late spring to early summer and late summer.
Height: 8 ft. • Prune light (2)
Zones: 4-9 • Sun / Part shade

'Kaeper' Early Large-flowered Group (1970 S. Franczak) Violet-blue with darker coloring along the midrib. Red anthers and white filaments make up the stamens. Flowers late spring to early summer and late summer to autumn.
Height: 6-8 ft. • Prune light (2)
Zones: 4-9 • Sun / Part shade

'Kakio' (Syn. 'Pink Champagne') Early Large-flowered Group (1971 K. Ozawa) Bright mauve-pink

'Jackmanii'

'Kaeper'

'Kakio'

sepals that are darker pink at the edges with yellow anthers. Flowers late spring to early summer and late summer.
Height: 6-8 ft. • Prune light (2)
Zones: 4-9 • Sun / Part shade

'Kasugayama'

'Ken Donson'

'Kardynal Wyszynski' Late Large-flowered Group (1974 S. Franczak) Beautiful dark crimson flowers with dark brown anthers. Flowers early summer to late summer.
Height: 8-12 ft. • Prune hard (3)
Zones: 3-9 • Sun / Part shade

'Kasugayama' Early Large-flowered Group (pre 1954 Sakurai) Lavender-blue flowers with a delicate overcast of pink and deep red-purple anthers. Flowers late spring to early summer and late summer.
Height: 6-8 ft. • Prune light (2)
Zones: 4-9 • Sun / Part shade

'Ken Donson' Early Large-flowered Group (1961 W. Pennell) Deep blue flowers with golden-yellow stamens. Beautiful seed heads. Flowers late spring to early summer and late summer to autumn.
Height: 8-10 ft. • Prune light (2)
Zones: 4-9 • Sun / Part shade

'King Edward VII' Early Large-flowered Group (c. 1902 Jackman & Son) Lilac-mauve shaded with pinks and blues. Flowers late spring to early summer and late summer.
Height: 6-8 ft. • Prune light (2)
Zones: 4-9 • Sun / Part shade

'Kirigamine' Early Large-flowered Group (Sakata no Tane Co.) Blue-violet with wavy margins and reddish brown anthers. Flowers late spring to early summer and late summer.
Height: 6-8 ft. • Prune light (2)
Zones: 4-9 • Sun / Part shade

'Kiri Te Kanawa' Early Large-

flowered Group (1986 Fretwell) The sumptuous, fully double, deep blue flowers with creamy yellow anthers are double on both new and old growth. Flowers late spring to early summer and late summer to autumn.
Height: 6-8 ft. • Prune light (2)
Zones: 4-9 • Sun / Part shade

'Konigskind' ('Climador') Early Large-flowered Group (1982 Westphal) Dark lavender blue with a lighter bar and dark red anthers. Flowers late spring to early summer and late summer.
Height: 4-6 ft. • Prune light
Zones: 4-9 • Sun / Part shade

'Lady Betty Balfour' Late Large-flowered Group (1910 Jackman) Deep purple-blue with contrasting creamy yellow anters. Flowers midsummer to autumn.

'Kirigamine'

'Konigskind'

Height: 15 ft. • Prune hard (3)
Zones: 3-9 • Sun

'Lady Caroline Nevill' Early Large-flowered Group (c. 1866 T. Cripps) Semi double, pale lavender flowers early. Single later. Best in part shade. Flowers late spring to early summer and late summer.
Height: 10-12 ft. • Prune light (2)
Zones: 4-9 • Sun / Part shade

'Lady Northcliffe' Early Large-flowered Group (1906 Jackman & Son) Royal blue with contrasting greenish yellow anthers. Flowers late spring to early summer and late summer.
Height: 6-8 ft. • Prune light (2)
Zones: 4-9 • Sun / Part shade

'Lasurstern' Early Large-flowered Group (1905 Goos & Koenemann) Deep, saturated lavender-blue with contrasting yellow anthers. Flowers late spring to early summer and late summer.
Height: 8-10 ft. • Prune light (2)
Zones: 4-9 • Sun / Part shade

'Lemon Chiffon' Early Large-flowered Group (pre 1992 E. Philips) Creamy yellow-white with yellow anthers. Sometimes a faint hint of a delicate pale pink bar. Part shade best. Flowers late spring and early summer and late summer.
Height: 6-8 ft. • Prune light (2)
Zones: 4-9 • Sun / Part shade

'Lilactime' Early Large-flowered

'Kiri Te Kanawa'

Group (1983 K. Pyne) Single and semi-double wisteria blue with magenta anthers. Flowers late spring to early summer and late summer.
Height: 8 ft. • Prune light (2)
Zones: 4-9 • Sun / Part shade

'Lincoln Star' Early Large-flowered Group (1950 W. Pennell) Raspberry pink with a deeper pink bar and reddish maroon anthers. Flowers late spring to early summer and late summer.
Height: 8-10 ft. • Prune light (2)
Zones: 4-9 • Sun / Part shade

'Lord Nevill' Early Large-flowered Group (pre 1875) Semi-double and single flowers of deep violet-blue with wavy edges and deep purplish red anthers. Flowers May-June and August-September.
Height: 8-10 ft. • Prune light (2)
Zones: 4-9 • Sun / Part shade

'Louise Rowe' Early Large-flowered Group (Mrs. J. Rowe) Very lovely, soft, pale-lilac flowers, single, semi-double and double. Best in part shade. Flowers late spring to early summer and late summer.

'Madame Édouard André'

Height: 8 ft. • Prune light (2)
Zones: 4-9 • Sun / Part shade

'Luther Burbank' Late Large-flowered Group (1959 Volosenko-Valenis) Purple-violet flowers with yellow anthers. Flowers early summer to late summer.
Height: 8-12 ft. • Prune hard (3)
Zones: 4-9 • Sun / Part shade

'Madame Baron-Veillard' Late Large-flowered Group (pre 1885 Baron-Veillard) Dusky-lilac-pink flowers with greenish anthers. Flowers midsummer to autumn.
Height: 10-12 ft. • Prune hard (3)
Zones: 3-9 • Sun / Part shade

'Madame Édouard André' Late

'Marie Louise Jensen'

Large-flowered Group (pre 1893 Baron-Veillard) Deep wine-red with contrasting creamy yellow stamens. Flowers summer to autumn.
Height: 8 ft. • Prune hard (3)
Zones: 3-9 • Sun / Part shade

'Maria Louise Jensen' Early Large-flowered Group (c. 1986 Westphal) Deep violet-blue with dark purple-red anthers. Usually single but sometimes semi-double or double on the previous year's growth.

Flowers late spring to early summer and late summer.
Height: 6-8 ft. • *Prune light (2)*
Zones: 4-9 • *Sun / Part shade*

'Marie Boisselot' Early Large-flowered Group (c. 1885 A. Boisselot) Pure white with golden yellow stamens and a satiny sheen. Flowers late spring to early summer and late summer to late autumn.
Height: 8-12 ft. • *Prune light (2)*
Zones: 4-9 • *Sun / Part shade*

'Masquerade' Early Large-flowered Group (1993 R. Evison) Mauve-blue flowers with a mauve central bar and dark red anthers. Flowers late spring to early summer and late summer.
Height: 10 ft. • *Prune light (2)*
Zones: 4-9 • *Sun/ Part shade*

'Matka Siedliska' Early Large-

flowered Group (1970 S. Franczak) Quite large, double white flowers with reddish-brown stamens on the previous year's wood. Single, white flowers later. Flowers late spring to early summer and late summer.
Height: 8-12 ft. • *Prune light (2)*
Zones: 4-9 • *Sun / Part shade*

'Matka Urszula Ledochowska' Early Large-flowered Group (1980 S. Franczak) White flowers with a pale green bar and deep red-brown anthers. Flowers late spring to early summer and late summer.
Height: 6-8 ft. • *Prune light (2)*
Zones: 4-9 • *Sun / Part shade*

'Miniseelik' Late Large-flowered Group (pre 1982 U & A Kivistik) Deep reddish purple flowers with a white bar. Flowers summer to autumn.
Height: 6 ft. • *Prune hard (3)*
Zones: 4-9 • *Sun / Part shade*

'Minister' Early Large-flowered Group (pre 1982 U & A Kivistik) Lavender blue with shading of purple and reddish purple anthers. Flowers late spring to early summer and late summer.

Height: 6 ft. • *Prune light (2)*
Zones: 4-9 • *Sun / Part shade*

'Miss Bateman' Early Large-flowered Group (1869 Noble) Charming rounded white flowers with a pale cream bar and dark red

'Matka Urszula Ledochowska'

'Miniseelik'

'Minister'

'Miss Bateman'

'Monte Casino'

'Moonlight'

anthers. Flowers late spring to early summer and late summer.
Height: 6-8 ft. • Prune light (2)
Zones: 4-9 • Sun / Part shade

'**Monte Casino**' Early Large-flowered Group (1975 S. Franczak) Velvety, reddish-purple with creamy yellow stamens. Flowers early summer and late summer.
Height: 8-10 ft. • Prune light (2)
Zones: 4-9 • Sun / Part shade

'**Moonlight**' Early Large-flowered Group (1947 M. Johnson) Pale, creamy-yellow with cream colored stamens. Part shade is best. Flowers late spring to early summer and late summer.
Height: 8-10 ft. • Prune light (2)
Zones: 4-9 • Part shade

'**Mrs. Cholmondeley**' Early Large-flowered Group (1873 Noble) Pale, lavender-blue with mauve veining and anthers of coffee brown. Flowers late spring to early summer and late summer to autumn.
Height: 10-12 ft. • Prune light (2)
Zones: 4-9 • Sun / Part shade

'**Mrs. N. Thompson**' Early Large-flowered Group (1954 W. Pennell) Deep, purple-blue with a vivid scarlet bar. Purple-red anthers. Flowers late spring to early summer and late summer.
Height: 6-8 ft. • Prune light (2)
Zones: 4-9 • Sun/ Part shade

'**Mrs. P.B. Truax**' Early Large-

'Mrs. P.B. Truax'

'Natascha'

flowered Group (1939 Jackman & Son) Periwinkle blue with pale yellow anthers. Flowers late spring to early summer and late summer.
Height: 6-8 ft. • Prune light (2)
Zones: 4-9 • Sun / Part shade

'**Multi Blue**' Early Large-flowered Group (1983 J. Bouter & Zoon) Deep, navy blue double and semi-double flowers. Spiky center. Flowers late spring to early summer and late summer to autumn.
Height: 6-8 ft. • Prune light (2)
Zones: 4-9 • Sun / Part shade

'**Myoojoo**' Early Large-flowered Group (1986 S. Arai) Velvety, violet-purple with a reddish-purple bar and golden yellow stamens. Flowers late spring to early summer and late summer.
Height: 6-8 ft. • Prune light (2)
Zones: 4-9 • Sun / Part shade

'Mrs. N. Thompson'

'Negritianka'

'**Natascha**' Early Large-flowered Group (c.1984 Westphal) Lilac-pink with a deeper mauve bar and reddish-purple anthers. Flowers late spring to early summer and late summer.
Height: : 6-8 ft. • Prune light (2)
Zones: 4-9 • Sun / Part shade

'**Negritianka**' Late Large-flowered Group (1964 Orlov) Dark, almost

black, velvety plum purple with red-purple anthers. Flowers midsummer to autumn.
Height: 8-10 ft. • Prune hard (3)
Zones: 4-9 • Sun / Part shade

'**Nelly Moser**' Early Large-flowered Group (pre 1897 Moser) Pale mauve pink with a deeper pink bar and dark red anthers. Part shade is best. Flowers late spring to early summer and late summer.
Height: 8-10 ft. • Prune light (2)
Zones: 4-9 • Part shade

'**Nikolai Rubtsov**' Late Large-flowered Group (1962 Volosenko-Valenis) Violet pink with a lighter central bar and yellow stamens. Flowers summer to autumn.
Height: 10 ft. • Prune hard (3)

'Perle d'Azur'

Zones: 4-9 • Sun / Part shade

'**Niobe**' Early Large-flowered Group (c.1970 W. Noll) Dark, velvety, ruby red with contrasting yellow anthers. Flowers late spring to early autumn.
Height: 6-8 ft. • Prune light (2)
Zones: 4-9 • Sun / Part shade

'**Omoshiro**' Early Large-flowered Group (1988 H. Hayakawa) White, boat-shaped sepals with pink margins and pink underside. Reddish pink anthers. Flowers early summer to late summer.
Height: 8-10 ft. • Prune light (2)
Zones: 4-9 • Sun / Part shade

'**Otto Fröbel**' Early Large-flowered Group (1865 Lemoine et fils)

'Nelly Moser'

Pearly white with lilac overtones aging to creamy white. Wavy margins and brownish red anthers. Flowers late spring to early summer and late summer.
Height: 6-8 ft. • Prune light (2)
Zones: 4-9 • Sun / Part shade

patens '**Yukiokoshi**' Early Large-flowered Group Double white with green overtones. A double form of the species Clematis patens. Flowers spring and late summer.
Height: 6-8 ft. • Prune light (2)
Zones: 4-9 • Sun / Part shade

'**Patricia Ann Fretwell**' ('Pafar') Early Large-flowered Group (1999 B. Fretwell) Early flowers are fully double, reddish-pink, fading to pink at the margins. The smaller inner sepals are pale pink and stamens creamy white. Single flowers later. Flowers late spring to early summer

'Piilu'

and late summer.
Height: 8 ft. • Prune light (2)
Zones: 4-9 • Sun / Part shade

'**Perle d'Azur**' Late Large-flowered Group (pre 1885 F. Morel) One of the most sought after clematis. The 4-5-in. flowers are mid-blue with a faint hint of pink on the midrib. Slow to establish. Flowers early summer to early autumn.
Height: 12-15 ft. • Prune hard (3)
Zones: 4-9 • Sun / Part shade

'Pink Cameo'

'Polish Spirit'

'Peveril Pearl' Early Large-flowered Group (1979 B. Fretwell) Pale lavender with soft pink tones along the midrib and light pinkish-brown anthers. Flowers late spring to early summer and late summer.
Height: 6-8 ft. • Prune light (2)
Zones: 4-9 • Sun / Part shade

'Piilu' Early Large-flowered Group (1984 U. & A. Kivistik) Pale mauve-pink double flowers with a deeper pink central bar. The double flowers are produced more regularly in the colder regions with a long dormancy. The flowers later in summer are single with the same coloring and wavy edges. Flowers late spring to early summer and late summer to autumn.
Height: 4-6 ft. • Prune light (2)
Zones: 4-9 • Sun / Part shade

'Pink Cameo' Early Large-flowered Group (1994 J. van Laeken) Soft pink sepals with a darker pink bar and pale yellow anthers. Flowers late spring to early summer and late summer.
Height: 8-10 ft. • Prune light (2)
Zones: 4-9 • Sun / Part shade

'Pink Fantasy' Late Large-flowered Group (1975 Fisk) Shell pink with peachy pink highlights and a deeper pink bar. Flowers summer to autumn.
Height: 6-8 ft. • Prune hard (3)
Zones: 4-9 • Sun / Part shade

'Pöhjanael' Late Large-flowered Group (pre 1981 U. & A. Kivistik) Purple-violet with a darker purple bar and white filaments and purple anthers. Flowers midsummer to autumn.
Height: 6 ft. • Prune hard (3)
Zones: 4-9 • Sun / Part shade

'Polish Spirit' Late Large-flowered Group (1984 S. Franczak) Velvety, deep purple with dark purplish-red anthers. Flowers summer to autumn.
Height: 12 ft. • Prune hard (3)
Zones: 4-9 • Sun / Part shade

'Prince Charles' Late Large-flowered group (1975 Keay) Pastel blue 4-in. flowers. Similar to Perle d'Azur more compact in growth. Flowers summer to autumn.
Height: 8-10 ft. • Prune hard (3)
Zones: 4-9 • Sun / Part shade

'Proteus' Late Large-flowered Group (pre 1876 C. Noble) Double or semi-double, dusky, lilac-mauve with shades of green on the midrib. Single flowers later. Flowers summer to autumn.
Height: 10 ft. • Prune hard (3)
Zones: 4-9 • Sun / Part shade

'Ramona' Late Large-flowered Group (1888 Jackson & Perkins) Pale lavender blue with dark red anthers. Flowers summer to autumn.
Height: 10 ft. • Prune hard (3)
Zones: 4-9 • Sun / Part shade

'Red Pearl' Early Large-flowered Group (pre 1992 K. Sugimoto) Wine red with pale lavender margins and creamy yellow anthers. Flowers late spring to early summer and late summer.
Height: 8 ft. • Prune light (2)
Zones: 4-9 • Sun / Part shade

'Rhapsody' Late Large-flowered Group (pre 1988 F. Watkinson) Sapphire blue with contrasting creamy yellow stamens. Flowers summer to early autumn.
Height: 8-10 ft. • Prune hard (3)
Zones: 4-9 • Sun / Part shade

'Richard Pennell' Early Large-flowered Group (1962 W. Pennell) Saucer shaped, rosy purple-blue, with prominent golden stamens. Flowers late spring to early summer and late summer to autumn.

'Ramona'

'Richard Pennell'

Height: 8-10 ft. • Prune light (2)
Zones: 4-9 • Sun / Part shade

'Roko-Kolla' Late Large-flowered Group (1982 U. & A. Kivistik) Creamy white with a greenish white bar. Flowers midsummer to early autumn.
Height: 6-8 ft. • Prune hard (3)
Zones: 4-9 • Sun / Part shade

'Romantika' Late Large-flowered Group (1983 U. & A. Kivistik) Deep dark-purple with greenish yellow anthers. The flowers appear almost black when they first open. Flowers early summer and late summer to autumn.
Height: 8-10 ft. • Prune hard (3)
Zones: 3-9 • Sun / Part shade

'Rosa Konigskind' Early Large-

'Rhapsody'

'Romantika'

flowered Group (1994 Westphal) Lilac-pink with wavy margins and dark purple anthers. Flowers late spring to early summer and late summer to autumn.
Height: 4-6 ft. • Prune light (2)
Zones: 4-9 • Sun / Part shade

'Rouge Cardinal' Late Large-flowered Group (pre 1968 A. Girault) Velvety, dark burgundy red with beige anthers. Flowers midsummer to autumn.
Height: 8-10 ft. • Prune hard (3)
Zones: 4-9 • Sun / Part shade

'Royalty' Early Large-flowered Group (c.1985 J. Treasure) Deep, blue-purple, semi-double flowers with yellow anthers on old wood and single flowers of the same color on new wood. Flowers late spring to early summer and late summer.
Height: 6-8 ft. • Prune light (2)
Zones: 4-9 • Sun / Part shade

'Ruby Glow' Early Large-flowered Group Ruby red with a paler bar and dark red anthers. Flowers early summer to late summer.
Height: 6-9 ft. • Prune light (2)
Zones: 4-9 • Sun / Part shade

'Rouge Cardinal'

'Snow Queen'

'Rüütel' Early Large-flowered Group (1982 U. & A. Kivistik) Large, dark purple-red flowers with pale purple filaments and brown anthers. Flowers midsummer to autumn.
Height: 6-8 ft. • No pruning
Zones: 3-9 • Sun / Part shade

'Satsukibare' Early Large-flowered Group (S. Uchida) Saucer-shaped, mauve-blue with reddish shades along the margin and with pinkish-purple anthers. Flowers late spring to early summer and late summer.
Height: 10 ft • Prune light (2)
Zones: 4-9 • Sun / Part shade

'Scartho Gem' Early Large-flowered Group (1962 W. Pennell) Single and semi-double flowers of deep pink with a darker central bar and

'Scartho Gem'

'Shooun'

pinkish-red anthers. Flowers late spring to early summer and late summer.
Height: 6-8 ft. • Prune light (2)
Zones: 4-9 • Sun / Part shade

'**Shooun**' Early Large-flowered Group (c.1967 Sakurai) Lavender-blue with deeper blue veins and contrasting yellow anthers. Flowers late spring to early summer and late summer to autumn.
Height: 8-10 ft. • Prune light (2)
Zones: 4-9 • Sun / Part shade

'**Silver Moon**' Early Large-flowered Group (1971 P. Picton) Silver-lilac blue flowers with creamy yellow anthers. Best in part shade. Flowers May-June and July-September.
Height: 10 ft. • Prune light (2)
Zones: 4-9 • Sun / Part shade

'**Snow Queen**' Early Large-flowered Group (1956 W.S. Callick) White with a mauve lilac tint and dark red anthers. Flowers late spring to early summer and late summer.
Height: 8-10 ft. • Prune light (2)
Zones: 4-9 • Sun / Part shade

'**Souvenir du Capitaine Thuilleax**' Early Large-flowered Group (1918 J. Thuilleaux) Long boat-shaped pink sepals with a broad, deep strawberry pink bar and golden brown stamens. Some detect a faint scent of violets. Flowers late spring to early summer and late summer.
Height: 6-8 ft. • Prune light (2)
Zones: 4-9 • Sun / Part shade

'**Special Occasion**' Early Large-flowered Group (1987 K. Pyne) Pale, pearly, pinkish-lavender with reddish brown anthers. Flowers late spring to early summer and late

'Sugar Candy'

summer.
Height: 4-6 ft. • Prune light (2)
Zones: 4-9 • Sun / Part shade

'**Sprinkles**' Early Large-flowered Group (2001 Spring Valley Greenhouses Inc.) Magenta red with a white speckled bar creating an overall sprinkled effect. Flowers late spring to early summer and late summer.
Height: 10-12 ft. • Prune light (2)
Zones: 4-9 • Sun / Part shade

'**Star of India**' Late Large-flowered Group (1864 T. Cripps) Four sepals of deep, velvety purple with a carmine bar and greenish anthers. Flowers midsummer to autumn.
Height: 10-12 ft. • Prune hard (3)
Zones: 4-9 • Sun / Part shade

'**Sugar Candy**' ('Evione') Early Large-flowered Group (1990 R. Evison) Pinkish-mauve with a deeper pink bar and yellow anthers. Flowers late spring to early summer and late summer to autumn.
Height: 6-9 ft. • Prune light (2)
Zones: 4-9 • Sun / Part shade

'Souvenir du Capitaine Thuilleax'

'Special Occasion'

'**Sunset**' Early Large-flowered Group (c. 1990 Steffen's) Velvety red with a hint of a darker red on the margins and yellow anthers. Flowers late spring to early summer and late summer.
Height: 6-9 ft. • Prune light (2)

Zones: 4-9 • Sun / Part shade

'**Sylvia Denny**' Early Large-flowered Group (1974 S. Denny) Double and semi-double, pure white, camellia-like flowers with yellow

stamens. Single later. Flowers late spring to early summer and late summer to autumn.
Height: 8-10 ft. • Prune light (2)
Zones: 4-9 • Sun / Part shade

'**Sympatia**' Late Large-flowered Group (1978 S. Franczak) Rosy violet with reddish purple stamens. Flowers early summer to late summer.
Height: 6-8 ft. • Prune hard (3)
Zones: 4-9 • Sun / Part shade

'**Syrena**' Late Large-flowered Group (1969 S. Franczak) Purplish, crimson-red with slightly wavy margins and golden brown anthers. Flowers early summer to late summer.
Height: 8-10 ft. • Prune hard (3)
Zones: 4-9 • Sun / Part shade

'Sympatia'

'Syrena'

'**Tateshina**' Early large-flowered Group (c.1986 Sakata no Tane Co.) Violet-blue with yellow anthers. Flowers late spring to early summer and late summer.
Height: 10-12 ft. • Prune light (2)
Zones: 4-9 • Sun / Part shade

'**Teshio**' Early Large-flowered Group (pre 1957 T. Kaneko) Beautiful, double, lavender-blue flowers with dark purple anthers. Flowers late spring to early summer and late summer.
Height: 6-8 ft. • Prune light (2)
Zones: 4-9 • Sun / Part shade

'**The Bride**' Early Large-flowered Group (pre 1924 Jackman & Sons) Pure white with pale yellow stamens. Flowers late spring to early summer and late summer.
Height: 8 ft. • Prune light (2)
Zones: 4-9 • Sun / Part shade

'**The President**' Early Large-flowered Group (pre 1873 C. Noble) Rich purple-blue with dark red anthers. Flowers late spring to early summer and late summer to

'Toki'

'Sunset'

autumn.
Height: 8-10 ft. • Prune light (2)
Zones: 4-9 • Sun / Part shade

'**Toki**' Early Large-flowered Group (1989 K. Sugimoto) Very full and rounded, pure white flowers with yellow anthers. The sepals have blunt tips that recurve and slightly wavy margins. Flowers late spring to early summer and late summer.
Height: 4-7 ft. • Prune light (2)
Zones: 4-9 • Sun / Part shade

'**Trikatrei**' Late Large-flowered Group (1984 U. & A. Kivistik) Satiny, dark violet with a paler purple bar and dark purple anthers. Flowers midsummer to autumn.
Height: 6-9 ft. • Prune hard (3)
Zones: 4-9 • Sun / Part shade

'**Tsuzuki**' Early Large-flowered Group (1982 K. Ozawa) Creamy

'Twilight'

white with a greenish bar and light yellow anthers. Flowers late spring to early summer and late summer.
Height: 6-9 ft. • Prune light (2)
Zones: 4-9 • Sun / Part shade

'**Twilight**' Early Large-flowered Group (1971 P. Picton) Mauve-pink with a deeper pink bar and greenish-yellow stamens.
Height: 8 ft. • Prune light (2)
Zones: 4-9 • Sun / Part shade

'**Unzen**' Early Large-flowered Group (pre 1957 T.Kaneko) Soft,

lavender-pink with a darker pink bar and purple-red anthers. Flowers late spring to early summer and late summer.
Height: 6-8 ft. • Prune light (2)
Zones: 4-9 • Sun / Part shade

___

'Valge Daam' Late Large-flowered Group (1980 U. & A. Kivistik) Bluish-white with a white bar and beige anthers. Flowers early summer to late summer.
Height: 6-8 ft. • Prune hard (3)
Zones: 4-9 • Sun / Part shade

___

'Vanessa' Late Large-flowered Group (1983 V. Denny) Smaller flowers of pale blue with a hint of pink at the base and creamy yellow anthers. Flowers midsummer to autumn.
Height: 10 ft. • Prune hard (3)
Zones: 4-9 • Sun / Part shade

___

'Veronica's Choice' Early Large-flowered Group (1962 W. Pennell) Double flowers of pale lavender with rosy lilac streaks and creamy yellow stamens. Single and semi-double flowers later on new wood. Flowers late spring to early summer and late summer.
Height: 8-10 ft. • Prune light (2)
Zones: 4-9 • Sun / Part shade

___

'Victor Hugo' ('Evipo007') Late Large-flowered Group (2002 Evison & Paulson Roser) Very deep violet with darker red anthers. Non-clinging in habit and evergreen in warm regions. Flowers early summer to late summer.

Height: 6-9 ft. • Prune hard (3)
Zones: 4-9 • Sun / Part shade

___

'Victoria' Late Large-flowered Group (1867 T. Cripps) Well formed, rosy purple with dark yellow anthers. Flowers midsummer to autumn.
Height: 10-12 ft. • Prune hard (3)
Zones: 4-9 • Sun / Part shade

___

'Ville de Lyon' Late Large-flowered Group (1899 F. Morel) Carmine red flowers with golden yellow

'Vanessa'

'Veronica's Choice'

'Vino'

stamens. Flowers early summer to autumn.
Height: 8-10 ft. • Prune hard (3)
Zones: 4-9 • Sun / Part shade

___

'Vino' ('Poulvo') Early Large-flowered Group (1970 Poulsens Nursery) Bright red with creamy yellow stamens. Flowers late spring to early summer and late summer.
Height: 10 ft. • Prune light (2)

'Victoria'

'Ville de Lyon'

'Violet Charm'

'Vyvyan Pennell'

'Voluceau'

Zones: 4-9 • Sun / Part shade

'Viola'

summer and late summer.
Height: 10 ft. • Prune light (2)
Zones: 4-9 • Sun / Part shade

'Viola' Late Large-flowered Group (1983 U. & A. Kivistik) Large, dark, violet-blue flowers with greenish yellow stamens. Flowers midsummer to autumn.
Height: 8-10 ft. • Prune hard (3)
Zones: 4-9 • Sun / Part shade

'Violet Charm' Early Large-flowered Group (1966 Solihull Nurseries) Pale violet-blue with reddish brown anthers. Flowers late spring to early

'Violet Elizabeth' Early Large-flowered Group (1962 W. Pennell) Pale, mauve-pink, double flowers with yellow anthers on old wood and single flowers on new wood. Flowers late spring to early summer and late summer.
Height: 6-8 ft. • Prune light (2)
Zones: 4-9 • Sun / Part shade

'Voluceau' Late Large-flowered Group (pre 1970 A. Girault)

Velvety, deep red with yellow stamens. Flowers early summer to autumn.
Height: 10 ft. • Prune hard (3)
Zones: 4-9 • Sun / Part shade

'Vyvyan Pennell' Early Large-flowered Group (c.1954 W. Pennell) Large, fully double, silvery purple-mauve with beige anthers on old wood and single flowers on new wood. Flowers late spring to early summer and late summer.
Height: 8-10 ft. • Prune light (2)
Zones: 4-9 • Sun / Part shade

'Warszawska Nike' Late large-flowered Group (1966 S. Franczak) Deep, velvety, reddish-purple with pale yellow stamens. Flowers early summer to late summer.
Height: 8-10 ft. • Prune hard (3)
Zones: 4-9 • Sun / Part shade

'W.E. Gladstone' Early Large-

flowered Group (1881 C. Noble) Well formed lavender-blue flowers with maroon anthers. Flowers late spring to early summer and late summer.
Height: 10-12 ft . • Prune light (2)
Zones: 4-9 • Sun / Part shade

'Westerplatte' Early Large-flowered Group (S. Franczak) Dark, velvety red with yellow anthers. Flowers late spring to early summer and late summer.
Height: 4-6 ft. • Prune light (2)
Zones: 4-9 • Sun / Part shade

'Will Barron' Early Large-flowered Group (1978 Clearview Horticultural Products) Clear mid-blue with soft yellow anthers. Flowers late spring to early summer and late summer.
Height: 8-10 ft. • Prune light (2)
Zones: 4-9 • Sun / Part shade

'Will Goodwin' Early Large-flowered Group (1954 W. Pennell) Pale lavender-blue with wavy margins and creamy yellow anthers. Flowers late spring to early summer and late summer.
Height: 8-10 ft. • Prune light (2)
Zones: 4-9 • Sun / Part shade

'W.S. Callick' Early Large-flowered Group (1983 Fisk) Bright red with dark red anthers. Flowers late spring to early summer and late summer.
Height: 10 ft. • Prune light (2)
Zones: 4-9 • Sun / Part shade

'Yukikomachi' Early Large-flowered Group (Kurasawa) Pale lavender margins with a white central bar and pale yellow anthers. Best in part shade. Flowers late spring to early summer and late summer to autumn.
Height: 8 ft. • Prune light (2)
Zones: 4-9 • Sun / Part shade

'William Kennett'

'William Kennett' Early Large-flowered Group (pre 1875 Jackman & Son) Deep mauve-blue with burgundy-red anthers. Flowers late spring to early summer and late summer.
Height: 8 ft. • Prune light (2)
Zones: 4-9 • Sun / Part shade

'Yamato' Early Large-flowered Group (1954 S. Arai) Deep purple-blue with a paler blue bar and dark red-purple anthers. Flowers early summer to autumn.
Height: 6-8 ft. • Prune light (2)
Zones: 4-9 • Sun / Part shade

MONTANA GROUP

A vigorous vine growing 20 to 35 feet. Produces masses of small, sometimes fragrant, white or pink flowers, in late spring to early summer. Flowers on previous season's growth. Not hardy to colder climates.

Height: 20-30 ft. • No pruning
Zones: 6-9 • Sun / Part shade

'Freda' (F. Deacon) Deep cherry-pink, 2-in. flowers with pale yellow anthers. Flowers late spring to early summer.
Height: 20-25 ft. • No pruning
Zones: 6-9 • Sun / Part shade

'Broughton Star' (1986 V. Denny) Semi-double, dark, dusky, reddish-pink flowers set off nicely against the bronze foliage. Flowers late spring to early summer.
Height: 20 ft. • No pruning
Zones: 6-9 • Sun / Part shade

'Jacqui' (mid 1990's J. Williams) Produces a mix of single, semi-double and double scented white flowers that have a hint of pink on the reverse. Flowers late spring to early summer.
Height: 20-25 ft. • No pruning
Zones: 6-9 • Sun / Part shade

'Elizabeth' (pre 1953 G. Jackman) Satiny pale pink, 2.5-in. flowers with a scent of vanilla and chocolate. Flowers late spring to early summer.
Height: 25-30 ft. • No pruning
Zones: 7-9 • Sun / Part shade

'Marjorie' (M. Free) Small, semi-double, greenish white turning creamy salmon-pink . Flowers late spring to early summer.
Height: 25-30 ft. • No pruning
Zones: 6-9 • Sun / Part shade

'Fragrant Spring' (1992 Proefstation voor de Boomkwekerij, Boskoop) Saucer shaped, light pink, 3-in. scented flowers set off against bronze foliage. Flowers late spring to early summer.

'Mayleen' (1984 Fisk) Satiny, pure pink, 2-in. flowers with a strong vanilla fragrance. Flowers late spring to early summer.
Height: 25-35 ft. • No pruning

'Warszawska Nike'

'Westerplatte'

'Will Goodwin'

Zones: 6-9 • Sun/ Part shade

montana 'Alexander' (1961 Fisk) Sweetly scented white flowers larger than most of the montana group. Flowers late spring to early summer.
Height: 25 ft. • No pruning
Zones: 6-9 • Sun / Part shade

montana var. glabrescens Creamy white, flushed with pink, strongly scented, 3-in. flowers. Blooms late spring to early summer.
Height: 20 ft. • No pruning
Zones: 6-9 • Sun / Part shade

'Mayleen'

montana var. grandiflora

montana 'Peveril'

montana var. grandiflora Masses of pure white, unscented, 2-3-in. flowers in late spring to early summer.
Height: 20-25 ft. • No pruning
Zones: 6-9 • Sun / Part shade

montana 'Peveril' (c. 1979 B. Fretwell) The 3-in., unscented, white flowers are held out on long stalks. The growth habit is less vigorous and better suited to the smaller garden. Flowers early summer to midsummer.
Height: 15-20 ft. • No pruning
Zones: 6-9 • Sun / Part shade

montana var. rubens 'Odorata' Pale pink sweetly scented flowers with bronze foliage. Flowers late spring to early summer.
Height: 20-25 ft. • No pruning
Zones: 6-9 • Sun / Part shade

montana var. rubens 'Pink Perfection' (pre 1952 Jackman & Son) Soft pink, 2-in. flowers with a strong vanilla scent. Flowers late spring to early summer.
Height: 25-30 ft. • No pruning
Zones: 6-9 • Sun / Part shade

montana var. rubens 'Tetrarose' (1960 Proefstation voor de Boomkwekerij, Boskoop) Bronze-green foliage offsets the large 3-in. scented, rose-pink flowers. Flowers late spring to early summer.
Height: 25-30 ft. • No pruning
Zones: 6-9 • Sun / Part shade

'Duchess of Albany'

montana var. wilsonii Sprague Small chocolate-scented white flowers that bloom later than other types in the montana group. Flowers midsummer.
Height: 35 ft. • No pruning
Zones: 6-9 • Sun / Part shade

'Pleniflora' (1980s Horn-Gfeller) Semi-double, greenish white with yellow anthers. Flowers late spring to early summer.
Height: 20 ft. • No pruning
Zones: 7-9 • Sun / Part shade

spooneri (Syns. c. chrysocoma var. sericea) White, 2-in. flowers, sometimes flushed pink down the center with blunt tips and graceful, wavy edges and creamy yellow stamens. Flowers are borne on long 7.5-in. flower stalks. Flowers late spring to early summer.
Height: 20-30 ft. • No pruning

crispa

Zones: 6-9 • Sun / Part shade

TEXENSIS-VIORNA GROUP

This group produces small flowers of extraordinary beauty. The flower form varies from pitcher-, urn- or tulip-shaped. They flower from early summer to autumn. Most are quite heat tolerant but some can be prone to mildew.

'Princess Diana'

'Lady Bird Johnson'

crispa (species) The small, fragrant, urn-shaped flowers are pale to deep violet-blue. The ends of the sepals recurve creating a very charming effect. The seed heads are also exceptional. Flowers early summer to autumn.
Height: 6-8 ft. • Prune hard (3)
Zones: 5-9 • Sun / Part shade

'Duchess of Albany' (1890 Jackman) Upward facing, tulip-shaped flowers of clear pink with a subtle darker pink bar. Flowers midsummer to late summer.
Height: 10-12 ft. • Prune hard (3)
Zones: 5-9 • Sun / Part shade

'Gravetye Beauty' (c.1900 F. Morel) Beautiful, deep ruby red, tulip-shaped flowers. Blooms midsummer to autumn.
Height: 10 ft. • Prune hard (3)

viorna

Zones: 5-9 • Sun / Part shade

'Kaiu' (1982 E. Pranno) Small, white bells tinges with pale purple. Flowers midsummer to late summer.
Height: 8 ft. • Prune hard (3)
Zones: 3-9 • Sun / Part shade

'Lady Bird Johnson' (1984 B. Fretwell) Dusky, purple-red, outward facing, tulip-shaped flowers with a crimson bar. Flowers midsummer to early autumn.
Height: 8-10 ft. • Prune hard (3)
Zones: 5-9 • Sun / Part shade

'Odoriba' (1990 K. Ozawa) Bell-shaped, pink with white at the base and greenish yellow anthers. Flowers midsummer to autumn.
Height: 8-10 ft. • Prune hard (3)
Zones: 5-9 • Sun / Part shade

pitcheri (species) Violet-purple, small urn-shaped, with recurving tips revealing a deep red on the inside of the sepals. Flowers early summer to autumn.
Height: 8-10 ft. • Prune hard (3)
Zones: 4-9 • Sun / Part shade

'Princess Diana' (1984 B. Fretwell) Elegant, outward facing, long tulip-shaped flowers of luminous pink with a slightly darker pink bar. Flowers midsummer to early autumn.
Height: 6-8 ft. • Prune hard (3)
Zones: 5-9 • Sun / Part shade

'Sir Trevor Lawrence' (1890 Jackman) Outward facing, tulip shaped flowers of carmine red with a darker red bar. Flowers midsummer to autumn.
Height: 8-10 ft. • Prune hard (3)
Zones: 4-9 • Sun / Part shade

viorna (species) Urn-shaped, thick red-purple sepals slightly reflex to reveal a creamy yellow inside. Flowers early summer to early autumn.
Height: 6-8 ft. • Prune hard (3)
Zones: 4-9 • Sun / Part shade

VITICELLA GROUP AND RELATED FORMS

Small-flowered, summer-blooming and disease-resistant only begins to tell the story of these supremely garden worthy varieties. What they lack in the size of flower they make up in sheer abundance of bloom and a graceful growth habit. This is perhaps the most heat tolerant group and is highly recommended for the warmer regions.

'Abundance' (c.1900 F. Morel) Semi-nodding, textured pinkish-red flowers with darker veining and creamy yellow anthers. Flowers

midsummer to autumn.
Height: 10-13 ft. • Prune hard (3)
Zones: 3-9 • Sun / Part shade

'Alba Luxurians' (c. 1900 r. Veitch) Bell-shaped, white flowers that open out with a distinctive splash of green on the tips and contrasting dark purple-black anthers. Flowers midsummer to early autumn.
Height: 12 ft. • Prune hard (3)
Zones: 3-9 • Sun / Part shade

'Betty Corning' (1933 B. Corning) Nodding, pale lilac, bell-shaped flowers that are sweetly scented. Flowers early summer to autumn.
Height: 10 ft. • Prune hard (3)
Zones: 3-9 • Sun / Part shade

'Black Prince' (1990 A.Keay) Semi-nodding, blackish, claret-red.

'Alba Luxurians'

'Betty Corning'

'Emilia Plater'

'Étoile Rose'

Flowers midsummer to late summer.
Height: 12 ft. • Prune hard (3)
Zones: 4-9 • Sun / Part shade

___

'Blue Belle' (1925 E. Markham)
Dark plum purple with creamy
yellow anthers. Flowers midsummer
to early autumn.
Height: 12-14 ft. • Prune hard (3)

Zones: 3-9 • Sun / Part shade

___

'Brocade' (1993 B. Fretwell) Light
red flowers shading to pink with
creamy yellow stamens. Flowers
midsummer to autumn.
Height: 12-15 ft. • Prune hard (3)
Zones: 4-9 • Sun / Part shade

___

'Emilia Plater' (1967 Franczak)
Pale blue with violet shadings.
Flowers early summer to late
summer.
Height: 8-10 ft. • Prune hard (3)
Zones: 4-9 • Sun / Part shade

___

'Entel' (1984 U. & A. Kivistik)
Pale, pinkish violet, deeply textured
with pale green-yellow anthers.
Flowers early summer to late
summer.
Height: 8 ft. • Prune hard (3)
Zones: 4-9 • Sun / Part shade

'Fairydust

'Étoile Rose' (pre 1903 Lemoine et
fils) Rose pink, nodding, bell-shaped
flowers. Flowers early summer to
autumn.
Height: 10 ft. • Prune hard (3)
Zones: 3-9 • Sun / Part shade

___

'Étoile Violette' (pre 1885 F.
Morel) Royal, dark purple flowers
with creamy yellow stamens. Flowers
early summer to late summer.
Height: 15 ft. • Prune hard (3)
Zones: 3-9 • Sun / Part shade

___

'Fairydust' (2001 Spring Valley
Greenhouse Inc.) Pale lilac with a
whitish bar. Flowers early summer to
late summer.
Height: 10-12 ft. • Prune hard (3)
Zones: 4-9 • Sun / Part shade

___

'John Treasure' (1999 Treasures
of Tenbury) Nodding, pagoda type
flowers of purple blue with a deeper
bar. Flowers early summer to late
summer.
Height: 10-12 ft. • Prune hard (3)
Zones: 4-9 • Sun / Part shade

___

'Kermesina' (pre 1883 Lemoine
et fils) Wine red, semi-nodding
with a blotch of white at the base of
each sepal. The anthers are almost
black. Flowers early summer to late
summer.
Height: 12 ft. • Prune hard (3)

'Étoile Violette'

'Madame Julia Correvon'

'Kermesina'

'Minuet'

'M. Koster'

'Little Nell'

'Mrs. T. Lundell'

Zones: 3-9 • Sun / Part shade

Zones: 3-9 • Sun / Part shade

'Little Nell' (pre 1914 F. Morel) Charming small flowers of creamy white edged in pale mauve. Flowers early summer to late summer.
Height: 12 ft. • Prune hard (3)
Zones: 3-9 • Sun / Part shade

'Madame Julia Correvon' (pre 1900 F. Morel) Rich, vibrant red with yellow stamens. Flowers early summer to late summer.
Height: 10-15 ft. • Prune hard (3)
Zones: 3-9 • Sun / Part shade

'Minuet' (c.1900 F. Morel) Semi-nodding, creamy white with pale purplish-red on the margins and yellow stamens. Flowers midsummer to autumn.
Height: 12 ft. • Prune hard (3)

'M. Koster' (1890's M. Koster) Deep mauve-pink with greenish yellow stamens. The sepals twist and narrow as the flowers open. Flowers June-September.
Height: 10-12 ft. • Prune hard (3)
Zones: 3-9 • Sun / Part shade

'Mrs. T. Lundell' (1985 K. Cedergren) Lilac rose tinged with purple. The sepals twist as the flowers open flat. Flowers early summer to late summer.
Height: 8-10 ft. • Prune hard (3)
Zones: 3-9 • Sun/ Part shade

'Pagoda' (1980 J. Treasure) The nodding, bell-shaped flowers are a very pale purple with mauve-pink on the margins. The sepals recurve

'Perrin's Pride'

'Pagoda'

and the flowers open to the shape of a pagoda. Flowers early summer to autumn.

Height: 10 ft. • Prune hard (3)
Zones: 4-9 • Sun / Part shade

'Perrin's Pride' (pre 1991 A. H. Steffen) Rounded, dark, dusky-purple flowers with anthers of greenish bronze. Flowers are larger than most others in the viticella group. Flowers early summer to late summer.

Height: 8-10 ft. • Prune hard (3)
Zones: 4-9 • Sun / Part shade

'Purpurea Plena Elegans' (pre 1899 F. Morel) Double, rosette-shaped flowers of dusky rose-purple. Flowers midsummer to autumn.

Height: 12-15 ft. • Prune hard (3)
Zones: 3-9 • Sun / Part shade

'Royal Velours' (pre 1914 F. Morel) Semi-nodding, velvety, dark reddish-purple with greenish black anthers. Flowers early summer to late summer.

Height: 10 ft. • Prune hard (3)
Zones: 3-9 • Sun / Part shade

'Venosa Violacea'

'Södertälje' (1952 M. Johnson) Reddish pink with green anthers. Flowers early summer to late summer.

Height: 12 ft. • Prune hard (3)
Zones: 3-9 • Sun / Part shade

'Tango' (1986 B. Fretwell) Creamy white edged and veined in red. Flowers midsummer to autumn.

Height: 10-12 ft. • Prune hard (3)
Zones: 3-9 • Sun / Part shade

'Royal Velours'

x triternata 'Rubromarginata' (1862 T. Cripps) Masses of hawthorn-scented, small, star-shaped flowers that are white with violet-red margins. Requires sharp drainage. Flowers midsummer to autumn.

Height: 15 ft. • Prune hard (3)
Zones: 3-9 • Sun / Part shade

'Purpurea Plena Elegans'

viticella

'Venosa Violacea' (1883 Lemoine et fils) White with broad purple violet margins and deep purple veining. The flowers are larger than many other viticella types. Flowers early summer and late summer to autumn.
Height: 10 ft. • Prune hard (3)
Zones: 3-9 • Sun / Part shade

viticella (species) A charming species of dark blue-violet, nodding flowers with pale green stamens. Flowers midsummer to autumn.
Height: 12-15 ft. • Prune hard (3)
Zones: 3-9 • Sun / Part shade

viticella subsp. campaniflora (species) Small, nodding, bell-shaped white flowers sometimes tinged with violet. Flowers early summer to late summer.
Height: 15-20 ft. • Prune hard (3)
Zones 3-9 • Sun / Part shade

OTHER SPECIES AND CULTIVARS

viticella subsp. campaniflora

'Anita' Tangutica Group (1988 R. Zwijnenburg) Small, bowl-shaped, white flowers with yellow anthers. Flowers early summer to autumn.
Height: 12-14 ft. • Prune hard (3)
Zones: 3-9 • Sun / Part shade

'Bill MacKenzie' Tangutica Group (1968 W. G. MacKenzie) Bright yellow, lantern-shaped flowers with red brown filaments and beige anthers. Attractive seedheads persist into winter. Sharp drainage required. Flowers early summer to autumn.
Height: 15-20 ft. • Prune hard (3)
Zones: 4-9 • Sun / Part shade

'Grace' Tangutica Group (1925 Skinner) Small, creamy white with pale wine-red stamens. Flowers midsummer to autumn.
Height: 12 ft. • Prune hard (3)
Zones: 4-9 • Sun / Part shade

'Golden Harvest' Tangutica Group (1990 Proefstation voor de Boomkwererij, Boskoop) Nodding, deep golden yellow, bell-shaped with deep purple stamens followed by large silky seedheads. Flowers early summer to late summer.
Height: 10-12 ft. • Prune hard (3)
Zones: 4-9 • Sun / Part shade

'Helios' Tangutica Group (1988 Proefstation voor de Boomkwererij, Boskoop) Bright yellow lantern-shaped flowers that open wide. Long blooming followed by an equally long display of seedheads. Flowers June-October.
Height: 6.5 ft. • Prune hard (3)
Zones: 4-9 • Sun / Part shade

intricata 'Harry Smith' Tangutica Group Small, nodding, broadly bell-shaped flowers of brownish purple outside and pale yellow inside. The foliage is bluish green. Flowers early summer to late summer.

Height: 10 ft. • Prune hard (3)
Zones: 5-9 • Sun / Part shade

'Lampton Park' Tangutica Group (1985 T. Bennett) Nodding, bell-shaped, bright yellow flowers with prominent yellow-green anthers followed by most attractive seedheads.
Flowers early summer to autumn.
Height: 12 ft. • Prune hard (3)
Zones: 4-9 • Sun / Part shade

'Bill MacKenzie'

'Helios'

tanguitica sbsp. obtusiucula 'Graveyard Variety'

terniflora

flowers adorn this fast growing plant making it useful as groundcover or to cover a fence or pergola in a hurry. Flowers early summer to late summer.
Height: 15-20 ft. • Prune hard (3)
Zones: 3-9 • Sun / Part shade

---

rehderiana (species) Pannicles of narrow, bell-shaped, pale yellow flowers scented of cowslip. Flowers midsummer to early autumn.
Height: 20-25 ft. • Prune hard (3)
Zones: 6-9 • Sun / Part shade

---

repens Finet and Gagnepain (species) Pale yellow, narrow, bell-shaped flowers drooping on stalks. Best when left to scramble and ramble on its own. Flowers midsummer to autumn.
Height: 12-15 ft. • No pruning
Zones: 6-9 • Sun / Part shade

---

tangutica subsp. obtusiuscula 'Gravetye Variety' Tangutica Group (1930's W. Robinson) Deep yellow, lantern-shaped flowers with dark maroon anthers. Flowers followed by attractive seedheads. Flowers summer to autumn.
Height: 15-20 ft. • Prune hard (3)
Zones: 4-9 • Sun / Part shade

---

tibetana subsp. vernayi var. vernayi 'Orange Peel' Tangutica Group (c. 1947) Nodding, lantern-shaped flowers of greenish yellow to yellow orange with purple-brown stamens. Foliage is grey-greenish blue. Prominent seedheads appear after flowering. Flowers midsummer to fall.
Height: 12-15 ft. • Pruning hard (3)
Zones: 6-9 • Sun / Part shade

---

vitalba (Old Man's Beard or Travelers Joy) (species) The name means white vine and so it is when covered with masses of small, scented white flowers. Not for the small garden. The fluffy seedheads are displayed well into winter. Flowers mid-summer to late summer.
Height 40-50 ft. • Prune hard (3)
Zones 3-9 • Sun / Part shade

---

williamsii A. Gray (species 1856) Small, nodding, bell-shaped, white flowers flushed with green. Flowers produced on previous season's wood. Flowers early to late spring.
Height 10 ft. • No pruning
Zones 7-9 • Sun / Part shade

'My Angel' Tangutica Group (1993 W. Snoeijer) Masses of small, nodding, bell-shaped reddish brown flowers that are bright yellow on the inside. Attractive seedheads. This is an aggressive grower and needs room to spread. Flowers early

summer to autumn.
Height: 6-8 ft. • Prune hard (3)
Zones: 4-9 • Sun / Part shade

'Paul Farges' ('Summer Snow') Vitalba Group (1962 Beskaravainaya & Volosenko-Valenis) Masses of small white

terniflora (species) Known as the "Sweet Autumn Clematis." A profusion of small, white, sweetly scented flowers are produced in late summer / autumn.
Height: 25-30 ft. • Prune hard
Zones: 5-9 • Sun / Part shade

Planting Instructions

1. Thoroughly water the clematis plant in its container at least one half hour before planting so the roots are fully hydrated.

2. Dig a planting hole at least 18 in. x 18 in.

3. Most soils, clay or sandy, will need amending. Mix in either aged compost, leaf mold or a soil booster to create a rich, loamy, well-draining soil. The ph can range anywhere from slightly acidic to slightly alkaline. It is a myth that clematis prefer alkaline soil conditions.

4. Large flowered cultivars should be planted so the top of the root ball is 3-4 in. deep beneath the soil line. With viable buds protected beneath the soil, the plant will be able to come back with new growth if damaged by animals, weather, or attacked by wilt. All other clematis types should be planted so the crown is at, or just below, soil level.

5. Carefully ease the plant from the container supporting the base of the plant with one hand. If the roots are heavily bound on the bottom gently tease them apart and place the plant in the prepared hole.

6. Sprinkle in a handful of bone meal and backfill with the amended soil.

7. Gently firm down by hand, water in thoroughly and top dress with 2 in. of mulch. The mulch should not bury or touch the stems of the plant.

8. Carefully monitor the watering of the plant. Young clematis must be kept moist and not allowed to dry out. The first two years are most critical while the root system is developing and not yet able to tap into moisture at a deeper soil level.

Pruning Instructions

GROUP 1 (NO PRUNING) Varieties in this group of winter and spring bloomers require no pruning. This includes members of the Atragene Group, Montana Group, and Evergreen Group. If pruning is needed to keep the plant tidy, take out dead or broken stems, or for general renewal, it should be done soon after the main period of flowering. This will allow the plant enough time to produce plenty of new growth that will provide flowers for the next year.

GROUP 2 (PRUNE LIGHT) Varieties in this group are principally the early large-flowered hybrids that bloom in late spring to early summer and again in late summer to autumn and the double flowering types. Pruning commences in early spring when the buds begin to swell and you can determine what wood is alive. First, prune out dead, diseased, broken, and weak stems. Then, starting at the top and moving down about a third of the height, prune just above a strong pair of buds on each stem. If there is a tangled mass of stems at the top, just cut below this, separate the stems, and tie to a support. After the first period of flowering is finished, give the plant another very light pruning and fertilize to stimulate the next round of blooms.

*We highly recommend that young Group 2 plants be hard pruned the first two springs after planting to help develop the root system and promote the growth of additional stems from the base of the plant. This is critical to the long-term development of a strong, healthy, multi-stemmed plant in this group. After the two years of hard pruning, you can return to the recommended light pruning approach recommended for this group.

GROUP 3 (PRUNE HARD) This includes the late large-flowering hybrids, Jackmanii-type hybrids, late-flowering species, the Viticella Group and its related forms, and the Herbaceous Group. They all bloom on the current year's growth (new wood) and require hard pruning in early spring when buds begin to swell. Start from the base of the plant prune just above the second pair of buds or about 12-18 in. from the ground. If the plant is herbaceous it may die back to the ground and if it is woody at the base, prune to a pair of buds just above the ground. The tangutica and orientalis types do not need to be pruned to the ground but can be pruned back to the main stems.

FERTILIZE AND MULCH CLEMATIS AFTER PRUNING

Always make sure the ground is moist before fertilizing. Clematis are heavy feeders and should be fertilized and mulched just after pruning in early spring using a balanced fertilizer. For varieties that provide a second period of flowering, another feeding is recommended just after the first period of flowering has finished. As a general rule, stop fertilizing once your plant is in bud with flowers and do not fertilize later than mid-August. A top dressing, lightly dug in around the base of the plant, of aged manure or bone meal in the late fall can also be quite beneficial. Plants in containers should be fed in early spring with a timed, slow release fertilizer and supplemented with a liquid fertilizer once a month.

Cut Flower List

Here are ten proven selections that will provide excellent cut flowers for the home gardener. Most clematis will make a good cut flower, but the following are easy to grow, require a minimum of training, and produce enough stems so you won't mind cutting them.

'Anita'
x diversifolia 'Blue Boy'
x diversifolia 'Heather Herschel'
x durandii
'Inspiration' ('Zoin')
'Pamiat Serdtsa'
'Paul Farges'
'Petit Faucon'
'Sizaia Ptitsia'
recta 'Purpurea'

Clematis By Color

Here are some of our most favorite and reliable varieties listed by color. These color lists are not comprehensive and are meant as a guide for the gardener who may be overwhelmed by the multitude of choices.

White

'Alabast' ('Poulala')
'Alba Luxurians'
'Anita'
'Arctic Queen'
'Candida'
'Duchess of Edinburgh'
'Hakuree'
'Henryi'
'Huldine'
integrifolia 'Alba'
'Lemon Chiffon'
'Marie Boisselot'
montana var. wilsoni Sprague
'Moonlight'
'Paul Farges'
'Snow Queen'
spooneri
'Sylvia Denny'
'White Swan'

Blue

'Arabella'
'Ascotiensis'
'Blue Light'
'Cecile'
'Daniel Deronda'

'Dorota'
x durandii
'Édouard Desfossé'
'Elsa Späth'
'Francis Rivas'
'Fujimusume'
'General Sikorski'
'H. F. Young'
'Ken Donson'
'Kiri Te Kanawa'
'Lady Northcliffe'
'Lasurstern'
'Lord Nevill'
'Maidwell Hall'
'Marie Louise Jensen'
'Multi Blue'
'Perle d'Azur'
'Prince Charles'
'Rhapsody'
'Shooun'
'Will Barron'
'Will Goodwin'

Lavender
'Belle Nantaise'
'Belle of Woking'
'Blekitny Aniol' ('Blue Angel')
'Claire de Lune'
'Countess of Lovelace'
'Fryderyk Chopin'
'Gladys Picard'
'Ice Blue'
'Ivan Olsson'
'Lady Caroline Nevill'
'Louise Rowe'
'Mrs. Cholmondeley'

'Ramona'
'Silver Moon'
'Tateshina'
'Teshio'
'Veronica's Choice'

Pink
'Alionushka'
'Asao'
'Broughton Star'
'Caroline'
'Charissima'
'Constance'
'Dawn'
'Dr. Ruppell'
x diversifolia 'Heather Herschell'
'Duchess of Albany'
'Étoile Rose'
'Foxy'
'Hagely Hybrid'
'Kakio' ('Pink Champagne')
'Madame Baron-Veillard'
'M. Koster'
'Markham's Pink'
'Mayleen'
montana var. rubens 'Pink Perfection'
'Pagoda'
'Pamiat Serdtsa'
'Pangourne Pink'
'Piilu'
'Pink Cameo'
'Princess Diana'
'Scartho Gem'
'Souvenir du Capitaine Thuilleax'
'Sugar Candy' ('Evione')

Red

'Abundance'
'Allanah'
'Ernest Markham'
'Gravetye Beauty'
'Kardynal Wyszynski'
'Kermesina'
'Madame Julia Correvon'
'Monte Casino'
'Niobe'
'Purpurea Plena Elegans'
'Rouge Cardinal'
'Ruutel'
'Ville de Lyon'
'Voluceau'
'Westerplatte'

Purple

'Aotearoa'
'Edomurasaki'
x diversifolia 'Eriostemon'
'Étoile Violette'
'Frau Mikiko'
'Gipsy Queen'
'Hakuookan'
'Helsingborg'
'Honora'
'Jackmanii'
'Negritianka'
'Petie Faucon' (Evisix)
'Perrin's Pride'
'Polish Spirit'
'Romantika'

'Sizaia Ptitsia'
'The President'
'Viola'
'Warszawska Nike'

Yellow

'Bill MacKenzie'
chiisanensis 'Lemon Bells'
'Golden Harvest'
'Helios'
'Lampton Park'
rehderiana
tangutica subsp. obtusiuscula 'Gravetye Variety'
tibtetana subsp. vernayi var. vernayi 'Orange Peel'

The Connoisseurs' List

These rare and hard to find varieties will be of special interest to the avid clematis collector.

'Anastasiia Anisimova'
'Anita'
'Andromeda'
'Black Prince'
'Black Tea'
'Blue Gem'
'Blue Eyes'
'Brunette'
'Colette Deville'
crispa
'Dark Secret'
'Denny's Double'

'Edward Prichard'
'Entel'
florida var. sieboldiana
'Grace'
'Jacqui'
'Kaiu'
'Lilactime'
'Pleniflora'
'Propertius'
'Red Pearl'
repens Finet and Gagnepain
'Sizaia Ptitsia'
'Tango'
viorna
viticella

Container

The plants in this list are well suited for use in a container. The container should be a minimum of 12 in. wide and 18 in. deep. Use a loamy, well draining potting soil with a neutral ph.

'Arctic Queen' ('Evitwo')
'Baltyk'
'Bella'
'Bees Jubilee'
'Blue Light'
'Brunette'
'Carnival'
x cartmanii 'Joe'
'Chalcedony'
'Crystal Fountain'
'Dawn'
'Edith'
'Édouard Desfossé'

florida var. flore-pleno
florida var. sieboldiana
'Fujimusume'
'Hania'
'Helios'
'Isago'
'Ivan Olsson'
'Kaeper'
'King Edward VII'
'Kiri Te Kanawa'
'Konigskind' ('Climador')
'Lemon Chiffon'
'Marie Louise Jensen'
'Miniseelik'
'Miss Bateman'
'Mrs. P.B. Truax'
'Multi Blue'
'Niobe'
'Petite Faucon' ('Evisix')
'Pamiat Serdtsa'
'Piilu'
'Põhjanael'
'Rhapsody'
'Rosa Konigskind'
'Royalty'
'Rooguchi'
'Sizaia Ptitsia'
'Special Occasion'
'Toki'
'Twilight'
'Unzen'
'Violet Elizabeth'
'Westerplatte'
'Yamato'

Clematis For Part Shade or North-Facing Walls

Clematis will not thrive in heavy shade or low-light aspects. Most clematis require at least half a day of sun or strong filtered light to flower well. Gardeners living in warm weather regions such as California that have long growing seasons, hot temperatures, and bright Mediterranean light can plant most clematis in a partial shade aspect and get good results. However, those living in the colder regions with a short growing season need to adhere more closely to the following recommendations. The following varieties are only some suggestions and by no means represent all the varieties that can be grown in partial shade.

'Alabast'
'Andromeda'
'Asao'
Atragene Group (all members)
'Bees Jubilee'
'Bella'
'Carnaby'
'Charissima'
'Claire de Lune'
'Comtesse de Bouchaud'
'C. W. Dowman'
'Daniel Deronda'
'Dawn'
'Doctor Ruppell'
'Edith'
'Elsa Späth'
Evergreen Group (all members)
florida var. sieboldiana
'General Sikorski'
'Gladys Picard'
'Guernsey Cream'

'Hakuba'
'H.F. Young'
'Ice Blue' ('Evipoo3')
'Ivan Olsson'
'John Warren'
'Lady Caroline Nevill'
'Lemon Chiffon'
'Louise Rowe'
'Masquerade'
'Matka Siedliska'
'Matka Urszula Ledochowska'
Montana Group (all members)
'Moonlight'
'Mrs. Cholmondeley'
'Nelly Moser'
'Omoshiro'
'Otto Fröbel'
patens 'Yukiokoshi'
'Peveril Pearl'
'Pink Cameo'
'Pink Fantasy'
'Silver Moon'
'Souvenir du Capitaine Thuilleax'
'Special Occasion'
'Sugar Candy' ('Evione')
'The Bride'
'Unzen'
'Violet Charm'
Viticella Group and Related Forms (all members)
'Will Barron'
'Yamato'
'Yukikomachi'

Captions

TITLE PAGE: 17th-century French limestone boar

PAGE 6: CHC oil and balsamic vinegar label

PAGE 7: Olive trees around the barn

TABLE OF CONTENTS: Image of olive oil label

PAGES 8-9: Old English staddle stones amongst oaks near the house

FOREWORD:
TOP, L-R: C. 'Ville de Lyon', C. 'Louise Rowe'
BOTTOM, L-R: C. 'Duchess of Edinburgh', C. 'Kaeper'

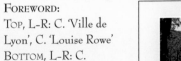

PAGES 10-11: Oak trees in spring and summer

PAGE 2: View towards the east from the deck through oak trees to the hills

PAGES 12-13: The pool area

PAGE 14:
Sculpture

PAGE 15:
Montage of wildlife, sculpture, and pasta bowl imprinted with CHC olive oil label.

PAGE 22: View through the pergola into the kitchen garden

PAGE 23: Montage of fruits from the kitchen garden

PAGES 16-17:
Dining arrangement with hydrangeas and C. 'Pamiat Serdtsa', C. 'Louise Rowe', C. 'Will Goodwin', C. 'H.F. Young', C. 'Proteus', C. 'Elsa Späth', C. 'Belle of Woking', C. 'Belle Nantaise'

The Farm | 2

PAGE 24:
TOP: C. 'Perle d'Azur'
BOTTOM: C. 'Elsa Späth' growing in the field under shade netting

PAGE 18:
Clock face near the CHC entry

PAGE 19:
Sunburst mirrors with collection of 1940s French ceramic cacti

PAGE 27: View of the barn from the growing field

PAGES 20-21:
Dining table at dusk and nighttime with arrangement of C. 'Marie Boisselot', C. 'Henryi', C. 'Elsa Späth', and C. 'Proteus'

PAGE 28: TOP: View of the barn through rambling roses, with red R. 'Chevy Chase' in the center BOTTOM: Rows of the English R. 'Swan'

PAGE 29: TOP: View of the barn and acetaia BOTTOM: Oak tree silhouetted in front of the barn at twilight

PAGES **30-31**: Views of the barn and detail of lightning rod

PAGES **38-39**: C. 'Gillian Blades' growing in a covered field

PAGE **32**: C. 'Henryi' growing under the shade netting

PAGE **33**: Rows of C. recta being cultivated for cut flowers

PAGE **40**: Rows of R. 'Polar Star'

PAGE **41**: Rows of R. 'Golden Celebration'

PAGE **34**: Rambling R. 'Seagull'

PAGE **35**: Open field of rows of C. 'Ville de Lyon'

PAGE **42**: Barrels in the Chalk Hill acetaia

PAGE **43**: CHC labels and bottles in shipping box

PAGE **36**: Rows of C. 'The President'

PAGE **37**: Details of C. 'Nelly Moser', C. 'Venosa Violacea', C. 'The President'

PAGE **44**: Plants in the greenhouse

PAGE **45**: Packing the clematis plants for shipping

PAGES **46-47**: CHC employees Maria Mendoza, Miguel Mendoza, Fernando Rueda, Arturo Pacheco, Jennifer Kesser

PAGES **54-55**: C. 'Henryi', C. 'Marie Boisselot'

The Flowers | 3

PAGE **48**: C. 'Pamiat Serdtsa', C. 'Pink Champagne', C. 'Henryi', C. 'Proteus'

PAGE **56**: C. 'Gillian Blades', C. x durandii, C. recta

PAGE **57**: C. 'Lasurstern'

PAGES **50-51**: C. 'Henryi', C. x durandii, C. 'Arctic Queen', C. 'Hakuookan', C. 'Louise Rowe', C. 'Marie Boisselot', C. 'Duchess of Edinburgh', C. 'Yukikomachi', C. 'Gillian Blades', C. recta, C. 'Elsa Späth'

PAGE **58**: C. 'Hakuookan'

PAGE **59**: C. 'Marie Boisselot', C. 'Henryi', C. 'Ville de Lyon', C. x durandii, C. 'Louise Rowe', C. 'Yukikomachi', C. 'Gillian Blades'

PAGE **52**: TOP, L-R: C. 'Louise Rowe', C. 'Marie Boisselot' BOTTOM, L-R: C. 'Henryi', C. 'Lasurstern'

PAGE **53**: C. 'Proteus', C. 'Lemon Chiffon', C. 'Pink Champagne', C. 'Multi Blue', C. 'Henryi'

PAGES **60-61**: C. 'Arctic Queen', C. 'Lemon Chiffon', C. 'Ville de Lyon', C. 'Pink Champagne', C. 'Nelly Moser', C. recta seedheads, C. t. 'Gravetye Variety'

PAGE 62: C. 'Nelly Moser', C. 'Ville de Lyon', C. *t.* 'Gravetye Variety'

PAGE 63: C. 'Marie Boisselot', C. recta seedhead

PAGES 70-71: C. 'Duchess of Edinburgh', C. 'Arctic Queen'

PAGE 64: C. 'Alabast'

PAGE 65: C. 'Arctic Queen', C. 'Duchess of Edinburgh', C. 'Paul Farges'

PAGES 72-73: C. 'Caroline', C. 'Claire de Lune'

PAGES 66-67: C. 'Marie Boisselot', C. 'Henryi'

PAGES 74-75: R. 'Polar Star', R. 'Seagull'

PAGES 68-69: C. recta, C. 'Paul Farges', C. florida *var.* flore-pleno, C. 'Ville de Lyon', C. 'Petit Faucon'

PAGE 76: R. 'Polar Star', R. 'Seagull'

PAGE 77: C. 'Anita'

PAGES **78-79**: C. recta seedheads, C. *t.* 'Gravetye Variety'

PAGES **86-87**: C. 'Arctic Queen', C. 'Henryi', C. 'Marie Boisselot', C. recta, R. 'Meidiland'

PAGES **80-81**: R. 'Golden Celebration'

PAGE **88**: C. 'Petit Faucon', C. 'Proteus', C. 'Pink Champagne'

PAGE **89**: C. 'Proteus', C. 'Pink Champagne'

PAGE **82**: R. 'Evelyn', R. 'Seagull'

PAGE **83**: R. 'Evelyn'

PAGE **90**: C. 'Henryi'

PAGE **91**: C. recta

PAGE **84**: C. 'Mrs. Robert Brydon', C. 'Lasurstern', C. 'Louise Rowe', C. 'Henryi', C. 'Lemon Chiffon', C. 'Ville de Lyon'

PAGE **85**: C. 'Lasurstern', C. 'Mrs. Robert Brydon', C. 'Louise Rowe'

PAGE **92**: C. 'Veronica's Choice', C. x durandii, C. 'Pamiat Serdtsa'

PAGE **93**: C. 'Ville de Lyon', C. 'Pink Champagne', C. 'Caroline'

PAGES 94-95: C. 'Lasurstern', C. recta seedheads, with C. 'Henryi' in background

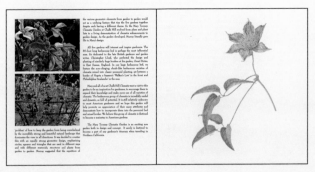

PAGE 102: C. 'Pamiat Serdtsa', C. 'Étoile Rose'

PAGE 103: C. 'Multi Blue' botanical drawing

PAGE 96: C. 'Ville de Lyon', C. 'Ken Donson'

PAGES 104-105: Mary Toomey Garden site plan

PAGE 99: C. 'Elsa Späth'

PAGES 106-107: Dr. Mary Toomey, entrance to garden, views of the herbaceous garden, C. 'Allanah'

PAGE 100: C. 'Multi Blue', C. 'The President', C. 'Paul Farges', C. 'Yukikomachi'

PAGE 108: CHC manager Murray Rosen

PAGE 109: View of the bench covered with C. t. 'Gravetye Variety', nepeta 'Walker's Low'

PAGE 110: C. 'Gravetye Beauty' botanical drawing

PAGE 111: C. 'Blekitny Aniol'

PAGE 118: R. 'Abraham Darby'

PAGE 119: C. 'Alionushka'

PAGE 112: C. 'Prince Charles' in fountain area

PAGE 113: C. 'Perle d'Azur' with R. 'Butterscotch'

PAGE 120: Seedhead botanical drawing of C. 'Gravetye Beauty' seedheads

PAGE 121: Seedheads

PAGE 114: TOP: C. 'Viola', C. 'Lady Northcliffe' BOTTOM: C. 'The President', C. 'Multi Blue', C. 'Louise Rowe', C. 'Paul Farges'

PAGE 115: C. 'Venosa Violacea'

PAGE 122: View of bench with C. t. 'Gravetye Variety' in flower

PAGE 123: View of bench with clematis seedhead

PAGE 116: C. 'Rooguchi', R. 'Albéric Barbier'

PAGE 117: C. 'Prince Charles'

PAGE 124: C. 'Viorna'

PAGE 125: C. 'M. Koster', C. 'Étoile Rose', C. t. 'GravetyeVariety' botanical drawing

PAGE 126: Botanical pencil drawing of C. 'Multi Blue'

PAGE 127: C. 'Caroline' arrangement in the Secret Garden

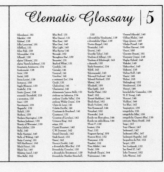

PAGE 128: C. 'Claire de Lune'

KAYE HEAFEY has always been drawn to nature, with a particular interest in flowers and floral arranging. A love of gardens and a "good eye" are traits with roots that go deep in her family. Her studies in art history formalized a love of beauty and developed her keen sense of aesthetics.

A new chapter in Kaye's life began with the creation of Chalk Hill Clematis. Part of her considerable founts of energy and imagination continue to be focused on the day-to-day running of the business. She considers herself very fortunate to have been able to turn a lifelong interest into a business – truly a blessing. Now, with the publication of *A Celebration of Clematis*, Kaye has reached yet another milestone.

RON MORGAN'S career in floral design began at age ten, when he won his first flower show competition in San Joaquin County in California. Over the course of his extensive career, he has designed window displays for Harrods and David Jones, opened retail floral and antique shops, consulted as an interior designer, conducted flower arranging classes, and, most importantly, become a highly sought-after speaker at garden club events around the world. He now lives in Alameda, California, and devotes most of his creative energies to the garden club lecture circuit. His first two books, *The Center of Attention* and *In the Company of Flowers* were published in 2002 and 2006, respectively. For a current listing of the times and places of his lectures and demonstrations, please visit his website at www.ronmorgandesigns.com.

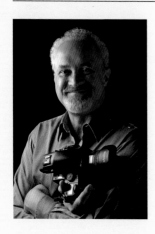

KEITH LEWIS' photography business serves a diverse clientele that ranges from commercial enterprises to private customers. A native of South Africa, he is based in Berkeley, California. For his portfolio and contact information, please visit his website at www.avideye.com.

MURRAY ROSEN is farm manager at Chalk Hill Clematis. An artist by training, he combines artistic flair with horticultural skill and knowledge. He works closely with Kaye Heafey on the management of the specialty cut flower farm and nursery. Murray was responsible for the extensive glossary of plants for *A Celebration of Clematis*.

RUTH CHIVERS is a UK garden writer and designer who has lived in California since 2002. In addition to being a book author, she is a consulting editor on *Garden Design* magazine, and writes a regular column for a leading UK consumer gardening title. A passionate garden visitor wherever she travels, Ruth also lectures on a range of garden subjects, including design and garden history. Ruth assisted Kaye Heafey with the text in *A Celebration of Clematis*.